W9-CJB-557

OSPREY
MILITARY

CLASSIC BATTLES

MILITARY
BOOK CLUB

NORMANDY 1944

Later in the morning of D-Day, men of 9 Canadian Brigade, the reserve brigade of 3 Canadian Division, disembarking from their LCIL (Landing Craft, Infantry, Large) and coming ashore rather more sedately at "Juno" Beach. Note the congestion on the very narrow strip of beach, left by the unusually high tide in the bad weather. The bicycles that the men are carrying were the most easily portable form of fast transport. (IWM photograph A23938)

CONSULTANT EDITOR: DAVID G. CHANDLER

OSPREY
MILITARY

CLASSIC BATTLES

THE MILITARY BOOK CLUB**

NORMANDY 1944

ALLIED LANDINGS AND BREAKOUT

STEPHEN BADSEY

First published in Great Britain in
1990 by Osprey, an imprint of
Reed International Books Ltd.
Michelin House, 81 Fulham Road,
London SW3 6RB
and Auckland, Melbourne,
Singapore and Toronto.

© Copyright 1997
Reed International Books Ltd.

All rights reserved. Apart from any
fair dealing for the purpose of
private study, research, criticism or
review, as permitted under the
Copyright Designs and Patents Act,
1988, no part of this publication
may be reproduced, stored in a
retrieval system, or transmitted in
any form or by any means,
electronic, electrical, chemical,
mechanical, optical, photocopying,
recording or otherwise, without the
prior permission of the copyright
owner. Enquiries should be
addressed to the Publishers.

Produced by DAG Publications Ltd.
for Osprey Publishing Ltd.
Color bird's eye view illustrations
by Cilla Eurich.
Cartography by Micromap.
Typeset by Typesetters
(Birmingham) Ltd, Warley.
Mono camerawork by M&E
Reproductions, North Fambridge,
Essex.
Printed in Hong Kong.

Wargaming Normandy by Richard Marsh.
Wargames consultant Duncan Macfarlane.

CONTENTS

Men of 9 U.S. Division taking cover before moving inland from "Utah" Beach on 10 June. Until the town of Carantan was taken "Utah" Beach was still in extreme range of German artillery. (IWM photograph EA25902)

THE ORIGINS OF THE BATTLE

The Battle of Normandy was the last great set-piece battle of the western world. Between June and August 1944, after the greatest amphibious invasion in history, armies of more than a million men fought in the tourist spots and picturesque farmland of northwestern France to decide the fate of Europe. For probably the last time in history, a British general led a mighty coalition into battle against an enemy that threatened the very existence of the European social order. If the Allies won, then the German occupation of France, which had lasted more than four years, would be over, and with it any chance of victory for Adolf Hitler's Germany. If the Germans could force a stalemate in Normandy, or even drive the Allies back into the sea, they would have at least a year in which to strengthen their defenses, turn against the advancing armies of the Soviet Union on the Eastern Front, and develop the secret weapons to which Hitler attached such importance. At worst, Hitler's Germany might, like Imperial Germany in 1918, sue for an armistice. At best, it might win the Second World War. What happened in Normandy would decide this: history has nothing to offer more dramatic.

Like many other great wars of history, the Second World War was actually a series of interlocking conflicts, which began and ended at different times and for different reasons. For most Europeans, it began through the attempts of Adolf Hitler, elected Chancellor of Germany in 1933, to extend German rule across Europe in a new empire, his "Third Reich," which by summer 1939 had already absorbed Austria and Czechoslovakia. On 1 September 1939, German troops invaded Poland, and two days later Britain and France declared war on Germany. But British defense thinking before 1939 had been based chiefly on naval and air power; for most of its land forces it expected to rely, as at the start of the First World War, on the French Army. France in turn had adopted a defensive strategy based on the Maginot Line, a formidable belt of fortifications built along its frontier with Germany. There was nothing that Britain and France could do to save Poland from occupation. After a failed attempt by British naval and amphibious forces to intervene against a German attack on Denmark and Norway in April 1940, the British government fell, to be replaced on 10 May by a coalition government under Winston Churchill, as Prime Minister.

By an improbable coincidence, it was also on 10 May that Germany launched a major attack on France through neutral Holland and Belgium, outflanking the Maginot Line. In the face of this the French Army, and with it British strategy for the war, collapsed in four weeks. By 3 June the last of the small British Army had been evacuated from France, mainly through the port of Dunkirk, and on 22 June France, uniquely among the countries defeated by Germany, signed an armistice. German troops would occupy northern France and the entire French coast, but the French colonies would continue to be governed by an unoccupied French state allied with Germany, with the town of Vichy in southern France as its capital.

This French collapse was the origin of the Battle of Normandy. If France were to be liberated, the British and their allies would have to reinvade and defeat the German occupation forces. Unfortunately in 1940 the British Empire had no allies, and only the German failure to win the Battle of Britain saved Britain itself from invasion, while Australia, New Zealand and India were all at risk from a potentially hostile Japan in the Far East.

On 10 June 1940 Italy, under Benito Mussolini, declared war against the collapsing France and against Britain, threatening Egypt and the Suez Canal from the Italian colony of Libya. Fighting in the Western Desert of Libya became, after the Germans reinforced the Italians with the Afrika Korps under Erwin Rommel, the major British land commitment, absorbing most of the British Army's fighting forces for the next three years. In April 1941 the Germans, having signed agreements with Hungary, Bulgaria and Romania, invaded Yugoslavia and Greece. As a result, the whole of Europe came under German domination, with only Ireland, Sweden, Switzerland, Spain, Portugal and Turkey remaining neutral. The British, although receiving arms and support from the neutral United States, were not remotely strong enough to consider an offensive strategy. Even if they had, there was no land front on which to conduct one except the strategically isolated Western Desert. The last, and by far the largest, battle of the desert war, at El Alamein in October 1942, between Generalfeldmarschall Erwin Rommel and Lieutenant General Sir Bernard Montgomery, was fought by no more than eleven divisions a side.

Hitler's Nazi Party was ideologically deeply opposed to Joseph Stalin's Soviet Union both on political and racial grounds. Nevertheless, in 1939 the two had signed a pact of friendship, and Soviet troops had participated in the invasion of Poland. On 22 June 1941 Germany, in company with all its allies, invaded the Soviet Union, occupying most of the country west of Moscow by Christmas. But the political collapse that had accompanied military defeat in other countries attacked by Germany did not happen. Instead, for the next three years, more than 200 divisions a side fought a bitter, often stalemated war for the occupied territories on a front stretching from the Baltic to the Crimea. It was here, on the Eastern Front, that the main land battles of the Second World War took place, leaving the Germans short of troops and equipment to deploy elsewhere. Neither side had any significant naval power or strategic aircraft, and virtually all their resources went into troops, tanks and guns. Almost at once, Stalin began to press the British for a "Second Front" to ease the pressure on his own forces.

On 7 December 1941 the Japanese attacked Pearl Harbor, declaring war on the United States and Britain. The Soviet Union remained at peace with Japan (not declaring war until a few days before the conflict ended in August 1945), but on 12 December Adolf Hitler, in one of the great strategic blunders of history, declared war on the United States. At the Anglo-American "Arcadia" Conference over Christmas 1941, the Americans decided that their war strategy would give priority to the defeat of Germany rather than Japan.

The events of 1941 gave the remainder of the war against Hitler its structure. Germany was committed to total war on several fronts against the Soviet Union, the world's largest land power, against the United States, the world's strongest industrial power, and against Britain, still the largest empire in history. The disparity in resources was such that no military skill could overcome it, and the political behavior of the Nazi Party made a separate negotiated peace with one of the Allies almost impossible. After Pearl Harbor the defeat of Germany, as Churchill put it, was merely the proper application of overwhelming force. This impressed itself deeply on the senior Allied commanders. By taking risks they laid themselves open to the sudden attacks of which the Germans were masters; but by caution – by never giving the Germans an opening – they were bound to win in the end.

The Germans, Soviets and Americans, sharing a common strategic heritage, saw the obvious Allied strategy as an invasion of France in 1942, or 1943 at the latest. The British opposed this notion of an early Second Front on both military and political grounds. Britain was already fully committed on four fronts: the Battle of the Atlantic, the war against Japan in southeast Asia, the strategic bombing offensive against Germany and the Western Desert campaign. Neither the British nor the Americans had the trained troops and equipment to undertake such a venture so early. Nor indeed had Churchill any desire to repeat the losses that the British had suffered conducting a major land campaign in France in the First World War. Instead, Churchill and his commanders convinced the Americans that the war should be fought where British troops were already deployed. In November 1942, just as Montgomery was driving Rommel back from El Alamein, American and British forces landed in French

North Africa, deep in Rommel's rear. In response, the Germans occupied the Vichy state, and its troops overseas joined the Free French as one of the Allies. By May 1943 the German and Italian forces had been pushed into northern Tunisia and forced to surrender. The American commander for the operation, which involved difficult negotiations with the French as well as the British, was Major General Dwight D. Eisenhower.

Whether an invasion of France could have been mounted, or succeeded, in 1943 remains controversial. Regardless, at the "Symbol" Conference in Casablanca in January 1943 the British again committed the Americans to a Mediterranean strategy. The Allies also agreed on a war aim of unconditional surrender for Germany. In June 1943 they invaded Sicily; Mussolini was overthrown by a coup d'état; and in September, as the Allies landed in southern Italy, the new Italian government surrendered. But German troops in Italy took over the defense of the country against the Allied advance, which was stopped south of Rome in November.

Also in January 1943, the Soviets had forced the surrender of the German Sixth Army at Stalingrad (modern Volgograd), and in July they had blunted the last great German offensive at Kursk. From then on they were able to maintain the offensive, gradually driving the Germans back. American war production, meanwhile, had reached full capacity, and trained American troops were pouring into Britain. Although Churchill continued to press for a Mediterranean strategy, the British, clearly now the junior partner in the alliance, finally bowed to American pressure for an invasion of northern France. At the "Trident" Conference in Washington in May 1943, a tentative date of a year ahead was set for the invasion, code-named Operation "Overlord." At the "Eureka" Conference with the Soviets in Tehran in November 1943 the Americans and British committed themselves fully to "Overlord," coupled with a second invasion of southern France shortly afterward. Finally, at the "Sextant" Conference in Cairo in December, the Allies named the now full General Eisenhower as Supreme Commander for "Overlord," to take up his post immediately.

Generalfeldmarschall Erwin Rommel, the man who more than anyone else was responsible for the German conduct of the Battle of Normandy. A publicity portrait photograph taken in 1943. Like his great rival Montgomery, Rommel was skilled in self-publicity. He agreed in 1933 to become the military adviser to the Nazi Party's paramilitary SA (Sturmabteilung) as a way of advancing his career. An expert on infantry tactics, he commanded Hitler's headquarters guard in the 1939 Polish campaign, after which he requested an armored division and achieved fame commanding 7 Panzer during the 1940 campaign in the west, before taking up command of the Afrika Korps. (IWM photograph HU17183)

THE OPPOSING COMMANDERS

The German Commanders

One of the abiding myths about the Third Reich is that it was brutal but efficient. In fact, Hitler actively encouraged bureaucratic conflict within the Nazi state in order to increase his own political control. By 1944, Germany's armed forces resembled not those of a single power, but of an alliance whose members functioned together rather less well than those of its enemies.

Hitler exercised daily control over the German armed forces as Oberster Befehlshaber der Wehrmacht, or Commander-in-Chief, through the Oberkommando der Wehrmacht (OKW). In December 1941 he also took over direct personal control of Army Headquarters, Oberkommando des Heeres (OKH), under which he placed all German forces on the Eastern Front, while German theater commanders other than on the Eastern Front were placed directly under OKW. From then on, OKH fought the war against the Soviet Union and OKW the war elsewhere, giving Hitler the power to adjudicate between them.

In May 1942 the aristocratic 67-year-old Generalfeldmarschall Gerd von Rundstedt was appointed Oberbefehlshaber West, or Commander-in-Chief of German forces in France, Holland and Belgium. By 1944, after the occupation of Vichy France, his OB West command was divided into a rear area and two army groups, each of two armies. Army Group G controlled Nineteenth Army, defending the southern coast, and First Army defending the southwest. In the north, Army Group B controlled Seventh Army, defending the coast of Brittany and Normandy, and Fifteenth Army, responsible for the remaining stretch of northern coast up to Antwerp. OB West's general armored reserve, Panzer Group West, was held back from the coast near Paris.

Despite this tidy structure, von Rundstedt would later observe that his only real authority was over the guard on his headquarters gate. In November 1943 Hitler gave Generalfeldmarschall Rommel a watching brief on all the coastal defenses, and command of Army Group B. As a former commander of Hitler's bodyguard, Rommel had direct access to Hitler over von Rundstedt's head. Panzer Group West, under General Leo Freiherr Geyr von Schweppenburg, came under OB West rather than under Rommel, but as a training command it had no authority to move its own troops. In March 1944 Rommel succeeded in getting three of its six armored divisions placed directly under him. The remainder, including I SS Panzer Corps under Obergruppenführer "Sepp" Dietrich, came except for training under OKW reserve, and could not be moved without Hitler's personal authority. Generaloberst Friedrich Dollmann, commanding Seventh Army, had no direct control over 21 Panzer Division, the only armored division in his area.

By spring 1944, Allied naval supremacy was such that, apart from raids by torpedo-boats and submarines, the German Navy played no part in the Battle of Normandy. The head of the German Air Force, or Luftwaffe, was also one of the most senior Nazi Party officials, Reichsmarschall Hermann Goering. Command of all aircraft in OB West area came under Generalfeldmarschall Hugo Sperrle's Luftflotte 3, answerable directly to Goering. In addition, the Luftwaffe had direct control over all antiaircraft guns, including the dual-purpose 88mm Flak gun, invaluable to the Army in its antitank role. Goering also controlled the supplies and replacements of all Luftwaffe troops in France, including parachute divisions, airlanding divisions and Luftwaffe field divisions.

A second private army within the Nazi state, also with direct access to Hitler, was the Waffen-SS, under Heinrich Himmler. Originating with the Schutzstaffeln or "protection squads" of the

General Dwight D. Eisenhower with General Montgomery (in the center) and Air Chief Marshal Tedder. Taken in Normandy at Montgomery's 21st Army Group Tactical Headquarters on 15 June, in Eisenhower's first visit to Montgomery after the D-Day landing. The son of a poor family, born in Texas and raised in Abilene, Kansas, Eisenhower was a West Point graduate who served as a major on the Staff in the United States in the First World War, and at the headquarters of Douglas MacArthur as Chief of Staff between the wars. In 1942 he became Chief of Operations under General Marshal (Chief of Staff), before being appointed to the North Africa command. Sir Arthur Tedder was by military standards an intellectual, being a graduate of Magdalene College, Cambridge. He joined the Army in the First World War, transferred to the Royal Flying Corps, and so into the RAF at the end of the war. He had worked with Montgomery as commander of the Desert Air Force, and friction had grown up between them through Tedder's feeling that Montgomery gave insufficient publicity and credit to his airmen. In the background can be seen Montgomery's two headquarters caravans, captured from the Germans during the Desert War. In one of these Montgomery hung a portrait of Rommel. (IWM photograph B5562)

old Nazi Party, this had by 1944 grown into a formidable military force, with armored divisions often stronger and better equipped than those of the Army. The Waffen-SS divisions, like the Luftwaffe divisions, were subordinate to Army command for operations but had their own chains of command and supply.

From OB West headquarters, therefore, von Rundstedt did not actually control his own air support, nor his antitank guns, nor his reserve armor, nor all of his infantry. He did not even control his immediate subordinate, Rommel. For practical purposes it was Rommel, through his better relationship with Hitler, who would command against the Allied invasion. Fifty-two years old and the son of a schoolmaster, he was a career officer who had associated himself with the Nazi Party as a way of rapid advancement. His first major command had been an armored division in France in 1940, and in leading the Afrika Korps he had developed a reputation for tactical brilliance – he excelled in the sudden counterattack. Yet, despite his skills and his many victories, he had yet to win a decisive battle.

However, even Rommel could not be described truly as the German commander in Normandy. In fact the holders of the key command positions at OB West, Army Group B and Seventh Army would all change twice before the Battle of Normandy ended. If any one person actually commanded in Normandy it was Adolf Hitler – from the maps at his headquarters at Rastenburg in eastern Germany. Whether, should the Allies invade, Hitler and OKW could respond rapidly enough to events across that distance was by no means certain.

The Allied Commanders

At the "Arcadia" Conference of December 1941 the British and Americans had established a joint command structure which was to last for the rest of the war. The service chiefs of both nations met as the Combined Chiefs of Staff and delegated to each of their Supreme Commanders absolute control over ground, air and naval forces in his theater of operations, regardless of nationality. For the next three years the two Allies worked

out the practical difficulties of fully integrated staffs. President Franklin D. Roosevelt, as Commander-in-Chief of U.S. forces, interfered little in the daily running of the war. Winston Churchill, in his self-appointed role as British Minister of Defense, kept in closer touch with events through the Chief of the Imperial General Staff, General Sir Alan Brooke. The command created for Eisenhower was SHAEF, the Supreme Headquarters, Allied Expeditionary Force. Fifty-three years old, Eisenhower had spent nearly his whole Army career on staff duties, never commanding anything larger than a battalion. He was essentially an administrator and a politician of formidable skill, whose main role would be to hold together a coalition that, as well as British and Americans, included Canadian, Polish, French, Dutch, Belgian and Norwegian forces. Eisenhower had also to balance the competing claims of the various armed services within the British and American forces, and to cope with the powerful personalities and opinions that inevitably accompanied command of such a large enterprise. In keeping with good inter-Allied relations, and with the immense importance of air support for the operation, Eisenhower's Deputy Supreme Commander was a British airman, Air Chief Marshal Sir Arthur Tedder, who had extensive experience in developing air-ground cooperation.

Under Eisenhower came the Allied force commanders. The Naval Expeditionary Force of Royal Navy and U.S. Navy vessels (plus ships from France, Poland, Norway and Canada), under Admiral Sir Bertram Ramsey, was to transport virtually all the Allied troops and stores to Normandy. The Commander-in-Chief, Allied Expeditionary Air Force, was also British, Air Chief Marshal Sir Trafford Leigh-Mallory. Under Leigh-Mallory came two tactical air forces, consisting chiefly of fighter-bombers: the RAF's Second Tactical Air Force, under a New Zealander, Air Marshal Sir Arthur "Mary" Coningham ("Mary" from Maori); and the U.S. Ninth Air Force under Lieutenant General Lewis Brereton. For the duration of "Overlord," SHAEF could also call upon the aircraft of the RAF's Air Defense of Great Britain (the former Fighter

Command), Coastal and Transport Commands, as well as the heavy four-engined strategic bombers of RAF Bomber Command and the U.S. Eighth Air Force.

Not all the Allied ground forces could cross to Normandy at once, and their command structure was designed to reflect this. Initially the landing force would be designated 21st Army Group and would consist of First U.S. Army under Lieutenant General Omar Bradley and Second British Army under Lieutenant General Sir Miles Dempsey. The commander of 21st Army Group, General Sir Bernard Montgomery, would also initially command all Allied ground forces in Normandy. Fifty-seven years old, Montgomery was a precise, methodical commander who believed in giving the enemy no chance at all. He had yet to lose a major battle and had already beaten Rommel three times. Vain and boastful, Montgomery infuriated others by often living up to his own boasts. His appointment reflected his reputation as the foremost fighting commander in the British Army.

When the Allied ground forces had been built up to a sufficient size, First U.S. Army would leave 21st Army Group and combine with the newly created Third U.S. Army to form 12th Army Group under Bradley, while First Canadian Army would join Second British Army under Montgomery. Eisenhower would then take over from Montgomery as ground commander, running the two Army Groups from SHAEF.

The weak link in this chain of command was between SHAEF and 21st Army Group. The autocratic Montgomery believed in being allowed to concentrate on the battle, and from his small headquarters paid little attention to superiors. Although he recognized Eisenhower's administrative abilities, Montgomery also held his ability as a strategist in low esteem. Once the invasion began, and the English Channel separated Montgomery from SHAEF, the potential existed for much misunderstanding.

THE OPPOSING ARMIES

The opposing forces in Normandy had many features in common. With some exceptions, troops on both sides were uniformed, disciplined conscripts in their twenties, sharing a common language and culture. Whatever his specialization, every man was trained to fight as an infantryman. The basic infantry weapons were bolt-action or self-loading rifles with ranges and rates of fire exceeding the needs of most firefights, which generally took place at under 300 yards. Only a minority of riflemen ever actually opened fire in combat. The basic social and tactical unit was a squad or section of about ten such riflemen plus a light or medium machine gun with a practical rate of fire of 200 rounds per minute. The most important adminis-

General Montgomery with Lieutenant General Bradley (on the left) and Lieutenant General Dempsey, taken beside Montgomery's staff car (note the American-style four-star car rankplate) at Dempsey's headquarters in Normandy, 10 June. In keeping with his reputation as "the GI General," Bradley is wearing the most simple of regulation officer's clothing with no rank badges visible except on the helmet. Dempsey is wearing a British paratrooper's smock (to which he was not entitled) with rank badges sewn on the shoulders over a normal senior officer's battledress. Montgomery is wearing his habitual, completely nonregulation uniform of brown shoes, light brown cord trousers, civilian light brown sweater and black Royal Armored Corps beret with two cap badges, one correct for his general's rank, the other the regimental badge of the Royal Tank Regiment (in which he had never served). (IWM photograph B5323)

trative unit, the focus of the soldier's immediate loyalty, was the battalion, of about 800 men, plus about fifty tanks for armor, twelve guns for artillery, and other vehicles according to specialization. The basic operational unit was the division of between 10,000 and 20,000 men, the smallest formation of all arms that could function independently on the battlefield. Divisions were switched as required between army corps, which had no fixed organization. Divisional structure was usually "triangular," with each formation commanding three lower formations. Less than half the members of a division belonged to the fighting arms, and very few troops of an army engaged in direct combat. A British infantry division at full strength of 18,400 all ranks needed 24,000 further troops at army corps level and higher to support it, but on the attack, "two up and one back," its actual front line would consist of 32 infantry sections, or fewer than 300 men.

The most numerous tanks in the Normandy campaign, the German Panzer IV, the American M4 Sherman and the British Cromwell, were all of broadly equal fighting value. All armies also had some form of slower, more heavily armored tank or self-propelled gun for direct infantry support. Artillery was of two main types: direct-fire anti-tank weapons with solid shot to penetrate the tank's armor, and indirect-fire high-explosive for general use. The infantry also carried shaped-charge weapons, such as the American Bazooka or German Panzerfaust, which could penetrate a tank's hull but had ranges of less than 100 yards. Direct air support was provided by single-seat propeller-driven fighter-bomber aircraft with an ordnance load of under 2,000lb (1,000kg) and top speeds of 400mph (650kph). Linking the whole structure together were portable radios, first used at platoon level in the previous year, enabling higher commanders to "listen" to a battle far too vast

The major difference in land warfare between the First World War and the Second World War was the existence of reliable, portable, voice communications radios, enabling even the highest commanders to talk with those in the front line. Without these, the resemblance of the Battle of Normandy to a First World War battle would have been even more pronounced. Here two corporals of 987 Field Battery, U.S. Artillery, receive instructions. Taken just inland from "Omaha" Beach, 10 June. (IWM photograph B5410)

The front line of a divisional attack. Men of 6 Battalion, Royal Scots Fusiliers, 15 (Scottish) Division, advancing through a smokescreen at the start of Operation "Epsom" in the Battle of Normandy, 26 June. Note that bayonets are fixed, and were surprisingly often used in close combat. Note also the reserve platoon about 200 yards behind these men. (IWM photograph B5953)

for one man to see. However, electronic warfare was in its infancy, and night or bad weather seriously reduced the fighting power of all ground and air forces.

The German Forces

The fighting doctrine of the German Army placed the highest possible stress on qualitative superiority in the front line. Win the firefights, it was argued, and the war would take care of itself. This doctrine reflected in the behavior even of the highest German commanders, who were brilliant operational leaders but indifferent strategists. The best troops, commanders and equipment went to the fighting arms of the combat divisions, which showed a marked superiority over their Allied equivalents. But by 1944 the strain of the war was causing the German divisional system to break down and be replaced as the basic operational unit by the battle group or Kampfgruppe, a force of all arms smaller than a division but with no fixed structure or size. Although its armored divisions were fully motorized, the rest of the German Army still depended heavily on horsed transport, with as many as 5,000 horses to a division.

In early 1944 the triangular German infantry division structure of 17,200 men in three regiments plus an artillery regiment was abandoned. The supporting artillery was reduced, and the infantry organized either into three regiments of two battalions or two regiments of three battalions, a divisional total of 12,800 men. The Luftwaffe's parachute divisions kept the nine-battalion organization. In Normandy most of the divisions

A Panzerkampfwagen Mark V Panther Model D, photographed in Normandy, July 1944. Developed by the Germans as their answer to the Soviet T-34, this tank came into service in 1944 and was first encountered in significant numbers by the Allies in Normandy. (IWM photograph STT4536)

defending the coast were "static" divisions with no organic transport, filled with overage or medically unfit troops. In compensation, some static divisions were given additional "Ost" battalions of prisoners of war from the Eastern Front who had "volunteered" to fight for Germany.

In 1941 the Germans had encountered Soviet heavy tanks for the first time, and as a result they had built their own, the Panzer V "Panther" and the Panzer VI "Tiger" and "King Tiger." These were impervious to most Allied tank guns at ranges greater than 200 yards and could knock out Allied tanks at five times that range. Panthers and Panzer

IVs equipped the armored divisions, while Tigers were concentrated in special heavy tank battalions. Additional firepower came from tracked assault guns, turretless tanks in all but name, crewed by the artillery. The basic armored division structure was 14,750 all ranks with one armored regiment of two battalions and two motorized infantry regiments, each of two battalions (three in the Waffen-SS, which was still largely a volunteer force). In practice, no two German armored divisions in Normandy had the same organization. A mechanized (panzergrenadier) division was nine battalions in half-tracks or trucks plus a battalion of assault

GERMAN ORDER OF BATTLE

OBERKOMMANDO DER WEHRMACHT (OKW)
Commander-in-Chief: Adolf Hitler
Chief of Staff: Genersalfeldmarschall Wilhelm Keitel
Chief of Operations Staff: Generaloberst Alfred Jodl

OBERBEFEHLSHABER WEST (OB WEST)
Generalfeldmarschall Gerd von Rundstedt (to 2 July 1944)
Generalfeldmarschall Günther von Kluge (to 18 August 1944)
Generalfeldmarschall Walther Model

ARMY GROUP B
Generalfeldmarschall Erwin Rommel (to 17 July 1944)
Generalfeldmarschall Günther von Kluge (to 18 August 1944)
Generalfeldmarschall Walther Model

Seventh Army
Generaloberst Friedrich Dollmann (to 28 June 1944)
Oberstgruppenführer Paul Hausser (to 20 August 1944)
General der Panzertruppen Heinrich Eberbach (temporary to 30 August 1944)

Panzer Group West (to 5 August 1944) **Fifth Panzer Army**
General der Panzertruppen Leo Freiherr Geyr von Schweppenburg (to 6 July 1944)

General der Panzertruppen Heinrich Eberbach (to 9 August 1944)
Oberstgruppenführer Joseph "Sepp" Dietrich

I SS Panzer Corps
Obergruppenführer Joseph "Sepp" Dietrich (to 9 August 1944)
Obergruppenführer Hermann Priess

II SS Panzer Corps
Obergruppenführer Paul Hausser (to 28 July 1944)
Obergruppenführer Wilhelm Bittrich

XLVII SS Panzer Corps
General der Panzertruppen Hans Freiherr von Funck

LVIII Panzer Corps
General der Panzertruppen Walter Kruger

II Parachute Corps
General der Falschirmtruppen Eugen Meindl

XXV Corps
General der Artillerie Wilhelm Fahrmbacher

LXXIV Corps
General der Infanterie Erich Straube

LXXXI Corps
General der Panzertruppen Adolf Kuntzen

LXXXIV Corps
General der Artillerie Erich Marcks (to 12 June 1944)

guns. A German division, therefore, could be anything from the five weak Ost battalions and four of sick men with no heavy weapons of 266 Static Division to the 21,386 fully equipped eighteen-year-old volunteers of the "Hitler Jugend" Division.

The Allied Forces

The American fighting doctrine was that wars are won by administration and organization. The best American troops went to rear-area positions, the less good to the fighting arms, the worst of all to the infantry. American training, firepower and industry, which was outproducing Germany in tanks by four to one, helped compensate for this. Divisions were designed as "lean" as possible, for highly mobile offensive operations. The basic American infantry divisional organization was triangular, with three regiments each of three battalions and an artillery regiment plus one heavy artillery battalion – in all 14,000 men. An armored division (including 2 French Armored, equipped by the Americans) was three battalions of M4 Sherman tanks, three of infantry in half-tracks and three of self-propelled artillery, plus supporting

---

General der Artillerie Wilhelm Fahrmbacher (temporary to 18 June 1944)
Generalleutnant Dietrich von Choltitz (to 28 July 1944)
Generalleutnant Otto Elfeldt

LXXXVI Corps
General der Infanterie Hans von Obstfelder

Armored Divisions
2 Panzer Division, 9 Panzer Division, 21 Panzer Division, 116 Panzer Division, "Panzer Lehr" Division

Waffen-SS Divisions
1 SS Panzer Division "Leibstandarte Adolf Hitler," 2 SS Panzer Division "Das Reich," 9 SS Panzer Division "Hohenstauffen," 10 SS Panzer Division "Frundsberg," 12 SS Panzer Division "Hitler Jugend," 17 SS Panzergrenadier Division "Goetz von Berlichingen"

Independent Armored Battalions
101 SS Heavy Tank Battalion, 102 SS Heavy Tank Battalion, 103 Heavy Tank Battalion (later renumbered 501-503 Heavy Tank Battalion), 654 Heavy Antitank Battalion, 668 Heavy Antitank Battalion, 709 Antitank Battalion

Infantry Divisions
77 Division, 84 Division, 85 Division, 89 Division, 243 Static Division, 265 Static Division, 266 Static Division, 271 Division, 272 Division, 275 Division, 276 Division, 277 Division, 326 Static Division, 331

Division, 343 Static Division, 344 Static Division, 346 Static Division, 352 Division, 353 Division, 363 Division, 708 Static Division, 711 Static Division, 716 Static Division

Independent Artillery Brigades
7 Werfer Brigade, 8 Werfer Brigade, 9 Werfer Brigade

Luftwaffe Divisions
2 Parachute Division, 3 Parachute Division, 5 Parachute Division, 16 Luftwaffe Field Division, 91 Airlanding Division

OBERKOMMANDO DER LUFTWAFFE (OKL)
Commander-in-Chief: Reichsmarschall Hermann Goering

LUFTFLOTTE 3
Generalfeldmarschall Hugo Sperrle

	Aircraft	Available (30 May 1944)
Day fighters	315	220
Night fighters	90	46
Bombers	402	200
Transport	64	31
TOTAL	891	497

III Flak Corps
About 120 to 160 88mm dual-purpose guns and 300 lighter Flak guns

Panzerkampfwagen VI Ausf E, Tiger, 1/sSS-PzAbt. 101. Illustration by David E. Smith.

Panzerkampfwagen VI Ausf E, Tiger, 3/sPZAbt. 503. Illustration by David E. Smith.

TANKS

	Armor (front/side)	Main Gun	Speed	Weight
USA				
M3 Stuart	44/25mm	37mm	40mph	13–15 tons
M4 Sherman	76/31mm	75/76mm	24mph	30–32 tons
British				
Churchill	90/76mm	75mm	15mph	37 tons
Churchill Mk 7	150/95mm	75mm*	12mph	41 tons
(* one regiment also with flamethrowers)				
German				
Panzer IV	80/30mm	75mm KwK 40	25mph	25 tons
Panzer V Panther	100/45mm	75mm KwK 42	34mph	45 tons
Panzer VI E Tiger	100/80mm	88mm KwK 36	23mph	54 tons
Panzer VI B King Tiger	180/80mm	88mm KwK 43	25mph	68 tons

Panzerkampfwagen Mark VI E Tiger, photographed in Germany in 1943, shortly after it had come into service. Developed as the answer to the Soviet KV-1 heavy tank, the Tiger was in service before the Panther and was first encountered by the Allies in North Africa. At first the Allies considered it too vulnerable to the superior mobility of their own tanks, and it had a reputation for mechanical unreliability. But in the close country of Normandy its threat greatly restricted the willingness of Allied tank crews to advance. The Allies estimated that it took them losses of up to three of their own tanks, with crews, to get one Tiger. (IWM photograph MH295)

arms that included a battalion of light tanks – in total 11,000 men and 248 tanks. The division provided three Combat Command headquarters (CCA, CCB and CCR for Reserve), enabling its battalions to combine into two or three battle groups as necessary. American doctrine retained a central pool of independent battalions of armor, infantry or artillery to be allocated to divisions as necessary, so that most divisions in Normandy were actually overstrength by two or three battalions. Infantry regiments often combined with armored battalions into "regimental combat teams" or RCTs. The American antitank artillery was about 40 percent towed guns and the remainder tracked self-propelled guns, both in independent battalions.

The British Army had no fighting doctrine as such, and an eccentric divisional organization. Principally a collection of independent infantry battalions as an armed police force for the British Empire, it recognized no real loyalty above the battalion's parent administrative organization, the regiment, which was not a fighting formation. Three battalions from different regiments com-

ALLIED ORDER OF BATTLE

SUPREME HEADQUARTERS ALLIED EXPEDITIONARY FORCE (SHAEF)

Supreme Commander: General Dwight D. Eisenhower
Deputy Supreme Commander: Air Chief Marshal Sir Arthur Tedder
Chief of Staff: Major General Walter Bedell Smith

21ST ARMY GROUP
General Sir Bernard L. Montgomery

Second British Army
Lieutenant General Sir Miles Dempsey

I Corps (to First Canadian Army 23 July 1944)
Lieutenant General J. T. Crocker

VIII Corps (from 16 July 1944)
Lieutenant General Sir Richard O'Connor
XII Corps (from 30 June 1944)
Lieutenant General N. M. Richie

XXX Corps
Lieutenant General B. C. Bucknall (to 3 August 1944) Lieutenant General B. G. Horrocks

Armored Divisions
Guards Armored Division, 7 Armored Division, 11 Armored Division (79 Armored Division)

Independent Armored Brigades
4 Armored Brigade, 8 Armored Brigade, 27 Armored Brigade, 33 Armored Brigade, 6 Guards Tank Brigade, 31 Tank Brigade, 34 Tank Brigade

Infantry Divisions
3 Division, 6 Airborne Division, 15 (Scottish) Division, 43 (Wessex) Division, 49 (West Riding) Division, 50 (Northumberland) Division, 53 (Welsh) Division, 59 (Staffordshire) Division

Independent Commando Brigades
1 Special Service Brigade, 4 Special Service Brigade

First Canadian Army (from 23 July 1944)
Lieutenant General H. D. G. Crerar

II Canadian Corps (from 12 July 1944 – from Second British Army 23 July 1944)
Lieutenant General G. S. Simonds

Armored Divisions
4 Canadian Armored Division, 1 Polish Armored Division

Independent Armored Brigades
2 Canadian Armored Brigade

Infantry Divisions
2 Canadian Division, 3 Canadian Division

12TH ARMY GROUP (from 1 August 1944)
Lieutenant General Omar N. Bradley

First U.S. Army
Lieutenant General Omar N. Bradley (to 1 August 1944)
Lieutenant General Courtney H. Hodges

Third U.S. Army
Lieutenant General George S. Patton Jr

bined into a brigade, and three brigades plus an artillery brigade into an infantry division of 18,400 all ranks. The armored division of 286 tanks (chiefly Shermans and Cromwells) and 15,000 men was divided into an infantry brigade of three motorized battalions and an armored brigade of three armored battalions – usually called regiments – plus an infantry battalion in half-tracks. A law unto themselves, individual battalions might be good or bad, and a commander who was skilled and lucky enough might combine them into a good division. But cooperation between battalions, and between infantry and armor, was notoriously poor. British close support for the infantry came from heavily armored Churchill tanks and from specially equipped tanks grouped administratively into 79 Armored Division, but dispersed throughout Second British Army. The most efficient and successful of the British arms was the artillery, organized so that even junior officers could bring down the fire of all guns within range upon a given target. The Canadians, who were all volunteers, and 1 Polish Armored Division, shared the British divisional structure.

Corps

V Corps
Major General Leonard T. Gerow

VII Corps
Major General J. Lawton Collins

VIII Corps (from 15 June 1944)
Major General Troy H. Middleton

XII Corps (from 29 July 1944)
Major General Gilbert R. Cook

XV Corps (from 2 August 1944)
Major General Wade H. Haislip

XIX Corps (from 12 June 1944)
Major General Charles H. Corlett

XX Corps (from 2 August 1944)
Major General Walton H. Walker

Armored Divisions
2 Armored Division ("Hell on Wheels"), 3 Armored Division, 4 Armored Division, 5 Armored Division, 6 Armored Division, 7 Armored Division, 2 French Armored Division

Infantry Divisions
1 Division ("Big Red One"), 2 Division, 4 Division, 5 Division, 8 Division, 9 Division, 28 Division, 29 Division, 35 Division, 79 Division, 80 Division, 82 Airborne Division ("All American"), 83 Division, 90 Division, 101 Airborne Division ("Screaming Eagles")

ALLIED EXPEDITIONARY AIR FORCE
Air Chief Marshal Sir Trafford Leigh-Mallory

RAF Second Tactical Air Force
Air Marshal Sir Arthur Coningham

73 fighter squadrons, 20 medium bomber squadrons, 7 army cooperation squadrons. Approximately 1,220 aircraft

U.S. Ninth Air Force
Lieutenant General Lewis H. Brereton (to 7 August 1944)
Major General Hoyt S. Vandenberg

65 fighter squadrons, 44 medium bomber squadrons, 56 transport squadrons. Approximately 2,000 aircraft

Air Defense of Great Britain
Air Marshal Sir Roderick M. Hill

41 fighter squadrons. Approximately 500 aircraft.

RAF Bomber Command
Air Chief Marshal Sir Arthur T. Harris

73 heavy bomber squadrons, 15 light bomber squadrons. Approximately 1,400 aircraft

U.S. Eighth Air Force
Lieutenant General James H. Doolittle

160 heavy bomber squadrons, 45 fighter squadrons. Approximately 2,400 aircraft

The M4 Sherman tank, the main battle tank of the United States Army, which also largely equipped the British Army and saw service in every theater of the war, including large numbers in service with the Soviet armed forces. Of the 88,410 tanks built by American industry during the war, 49,234 were variants of the Sherman. Mechanically reliable, it had a bad reputation for catching fire easily, and was no match for the heavier German tanks. This particular example is a Chrysler M4A4 Sherman serving with 1 Polish Armored Division in France in July 1944, and shows two of the devices used to improve the Sherman when facing heavier German tanks. The first is the fitting of spare track links, bogey wheels, and other metal to the frontal hull armor of the tank. The other is a British development, the replacement of the 75mm gun with a 17pdr antitank gun. Called "Fireflies," one Sherman in four in British armored units was so equipped. The drawback to the 17pdr was that it had no high-explosive round developed until September 1944. The Americans began to replace their 75mm guns with the new 76mm in July 1944, but in the Battle of Normandy the 76mm gun was found to be no more effective than its predecessor. (IWM photograph B7573)

M4AI, 3rd Platoon, "D" Company of 66th or 67th Armored Regiment, U.S. 2nd Armored Division; Cotentin Peninsula. Illustration by Steven J. Zaloga.

ASSAULT GUNS/TANK DESTROYERS

	Armor (front/side)	Main Gun	Speed	Weight
USA				
M10 Wolverine	76/51mm	3in	24mph	32 tons
M18 Hellcat	50/25mm	76mm	50mph	20 tons
German				
Jagdpanther	80/50mm	88mm KwK 43	34mph	46 tons
Jagdtiger	250/80mm	128mm PaK 44	23mph	70 tons

Not a tank but an American M10 Wolverine tank destroyer, this particular one in British service, part of 13/18 Hussars, 27 Armored Brigade, on "Sword" Beach on D-Day, 6 June 1944. The M10 was a Sherman chassis with a 3in antitank gun fitted in a turret. The Americans formed a separate Antitank Command in November 1941 and renamed it Tank Destroyer Command a few days later. (IWM photograph B5086)

THE OPPOSING PLANS

There was nothing inevitable about the Allied victory in Normandy. In late spring 1944 the German Army consisted of 314 divisions of which 47 were armored, plus 66 divisions belonging to various allies. Of these, 215 divisions were deployed on the Eastern Front, 36 in the Balkans, 27 in Scandinavia, 25 in Italy, and 8 in transit between fronts, with no strategic reserve. This left 61 divisions, of which 11 were armored, to defend France. Allowing for the weakness of German divisions and the strength of the Allies, this was roughly equal to the entire Allied force for Operation "Overlord," and could have been more than enough to defeat the invasion.

The Germans' Plans

Because there was no single supreme German commander in the west, there was no unified plan to repel the invaders. Adolf Hitler's view was that the Allies would attack by the most direct route, at the Pas de Calais, in the fine weather of late June or early July. As commander of Panzer Group West, General Geyr von Schweppenburg wanted his armored divisions grouped back from the coast to counterattack the Allies as they advanced inland. Twice before, the Allies had seen successful amphibious invasions turned into delayed and stalemated slogging matches by German operational skill: it had taken five months to defeat the German forces in North Africa; while the capture of Rome, expected to take place in November 1943, was not achieved until 4 June 1944. Generalfeldmarschall von Rundstedt endorsed his subordinate's strategy for a flexible defense, and was later to say that if he had been allowed a free hand he would have made the Allies pay terribly for their victory.

This strategy was firmly opposed by Generalfeldmarschall Rommel. From his own experiences in North Africa, he did not believe that such a mobile defense was possible under conditions of Allied air superiority, which were necessary for them even to consider invasion. Rommel believed that the Pas de Calais was the most likely Allied invasion point, but that the only German chance was to defeat the invasion before it had really happened, on the beaches in the first 24 hours. To this end he pressed repeatedly for the German armor to be deployed close to the beaches under his own control. In May 1944 he also petitioned Goering to concentrate the guns of III Flak Corps in northern France close to the beaches, but without success.

Neither Goering nor Rommel knew it, but the Luftwaffe was actually providing the Allies with extremely valuable information. The most prized and secret possession of Allied signals intelligence was "Ultra," based on a primitive British computer capable of breaking the top-secret German "Enigma" codes, a mechanical system used to transmit their most valued signals. In early sum-

A typical German pillbox along the Normandy coast. This one is on "Gold" Beach, and the photograph was taken a month after its capture by the British (note the White Ensign flag). Although the pillbox has been struck repeatedly by Allied antitank shells, none appears to have penetrated. The scorching around the entrance suggests that either a satchel charge or a flamethrower has been used. (IWM photograph B6381)

Improvised beach defenses constructed on Rommel's orders between January and June 1944 along the invasion coast. These particular defenses are in the Pas de Calais area in May, and their size can be judged from the men running for cover as the RAF reconnaissance Spitfire makes a very low pass. The steel girders were meant as tank traps and often had mines fitted to them. This was no substitute for the Atlantic Wall of German propaganda. (IWM photograph CL1)

mer 1944 the only "Enigma" transmissions being broken regularly by "Ultra" were those of the Luftwaffe, including all its fighting divisions and its liaison officers at other divisional headquarters. So long as the front was static, however, most German transmissions were sent by land lines, where not even "Ultra" could reach them.

The Allies' Plans

Since May 1943, COSSAC (Chief of Staff to the Supreme Allied Commander) Headquarters, the forerunner of SHAEF, had been studying the invasion problem. Classical strategy favored the most direct invasion route, across the Strait of Dover. It was here that the Atlantic Wall, the fortification built by the Germans along the coast, was at its strongest. It was also here that Fifteenth Army with its seventeen divisions was stationed. COSSAC instead decided on Normandy, which was defended by Seventh Army with eleven divisions. The disastrous Dieppe raid in August 1942 had shown that a port could not be captured in the initial landings. Instead prefabricated harbors, code-named "Mulberry," were built to be towed in sections across the Channel.

Any chance of Allied victory depended on their landing troops and supplies in Normandy faster than the Germans could reinforce their front.

A Mulberry harbor. This picture shows the completed British Mulberry off the coast of Arromanches in September 1944, by which time its usefulness was largely over. (IWM photograph BU1029)

Apart from efficient administration, this would depend on two factors. The first was a major deception plan, Operation "Fortitude," to convince the Germans that the SHAEF forces were twice their actual size. Double agents, fake radio transmissions, dummy encampments and planted news stories all created the illusion of FUSAG, or First U.S. Army Group, a force of 30 divisions in southeast England under the flamboyant Lieutenant General George S. Patton. Even after D-Day for "Overlord," set for 5 June 1944, the Allies hoped to convince the Germans that FUSAG was still waiting to invade the Pas de Calais area in July, so pinning Fifteenth Army in place. The other main requirement was air superiority. In January 1944, Air Chief Marshal Leigh–Mallory announced a plan for all available

aircraft to attack the French transport and railway system. This had two objectives: to prevent the easy movement of German troops to the battlefield, and to force Luftflotte 3 into defending the railways, thereby entering a battle of attrition that it would then lose. RAF Bomber Command and the U.S. Eighth Air Force were, as throughout the war, reluctant to be distracted from their preferred strategy of bombing German cities. But, after lengthy negotiations, Eisenhower obtained formal control of the heavy bombers on 15 April. Thereafter, the Allied air forces smashed both the French railway system, which was reduced to 40 percent capacity, and the Luftwaffe in the west. By D-Day they had virtual air supremacy over France by day and by night.

As ground commander, the plan for how the

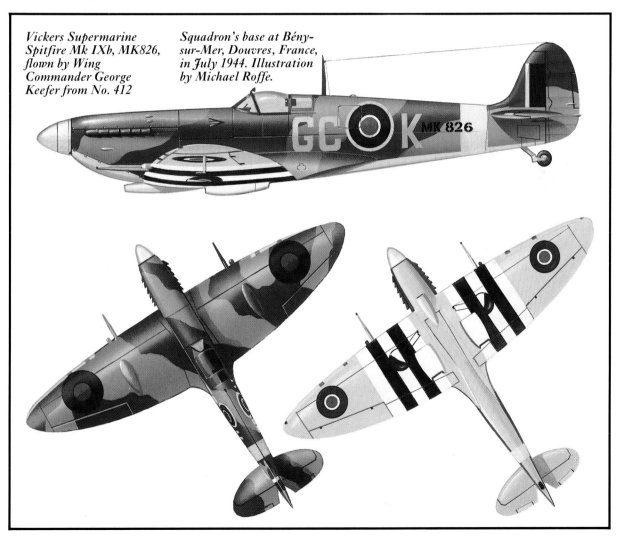

Vickers Supermarine Spitfire Mk IXb, MK826, flown by Wing Commander George Keefer from No. 412 Squadron's base at Bény-sur-Mer, Douvres, France, in July 1944. Illustration by Michael Roffe.

ALLIED BOMBERS

	Maximum speed (mph)	Ceiling (ft)	Bomb load (lb)	Range (miles)	Crew
USA					
B–17 Flying Fortress	317	36,600	4,000	2,850	10
B-24 Liberator	300	38,000	4,000	2,000	10
B-25 Mitchell	292	24,200	4,000	1,660	5
B-26 Marauder	285	21,700	4,000	1,100*	6
A-20 Havoc	325	24,250	2,000	250	3

(a version of the Havoc in RAF service was known as the Boston)

British					
Lancaster	287	20,000	14,000	1,660	7
Halifax	280	20,000	13,000	980	7
Mosquito	370	32,000	2,000	1,270	2

ALLIED FIGHTERS AND FIGHTER BOMBERS (single seat)

	Maximum speed (mph)	Ceiling (ft)	Armament (cannon/machine guns)	Range (miles)
USA				
P-38 Lightning	414	44,000	1x20mm/4x0.5in*	450
P-47 Thunderbolt	467	43,000	8x0.5in*	2,200**
P-51 Mustang	437	41,900	6x0.5in*	2,300**
British				
Spitfire	448	44,500	4x20mm*	850
Typhoon	405	34,000	4x20mm*	610

*All these had underwing attachments for two to three 500lb bombs or eight to ten 60lb unguided rockets. The Typhoon in particular became famous for its rocket attacks against enemy armor. **With external drop tanks.

The battle for air superiority over France. B-26 Marauders of U.S. Ninth Air Force attacking Valenciennes railway yard on 2 May 1944. Between 9 February and 6 June, Allied air forces flew 21,949 sorties and dropped 76,200 tons of bombs on more than 800 different transport targets in France. The Fighting French (as the Free French had renamed themselves) agreed to accept the heavy French civilian casualties caused by this strategy. (IWM photograph EA21615)

Allied landing craft waiting at Southampton Docks on 1 June. Note the bow door ramps of the LCT (Landing Craft, Tank) and the extra radio equipment of the LCH (Landing Craft, Headquarters). Altogether some 7,000 vessels, including 4,126 landing ships and landing craft, were involved in operations on D-Day. Two extra staff complexes, BUCO (Build Up Control) and TURCO (Turn Round Control) had to be created by SHAEF to coordinate the movement of troops across the English Channel. (IWM photograph A23731)

battle would develop was worked out by Montgomery, and finalized at a general SHAEF briefing on 15 May. The British would land in eastern Normandy and the Americans to their west, after which both would advance deep inland. The Germans would fight a mobile, flexible defensive battle (as desired by Geyr von Schweppenburg), holding their armor back for a counterstroke. The British, regarded by the Germans as the best of the Allied troops, would push down to the Caen-Falaise plain, apparently threatening to break out toward Paris by the most direct route, with the Americans covering their flank and rear. But this breakout attempt would be a feint. After the Germans had reinforced against it the Americans would break out of Normandy, turning westward to secure the ports of Brittany. These, with Cherbourg, would give the Allies a strong logistics base for the next stage. All four Allied armies would then turn eastward and advance on a broad front, denying the Germans the opening for a counterstroke against a flank. Although the battle had no fixed timetable, the Allies expected to be substantially inland by the end of June, to have reached the Seine River at about D-Day plus 90 days, and that the war would end in the following spring.

At the start of June, ominously, the weather in southern England and northern France was very bad, and on the morning of 4 June the invasion was delayed for 24 hours in the hope of an improvement. At 2145 hours on 4 June, after consulting his meteorologists and the SHAEF commanders, Eisenhower came to a decision: on 6 June 1944 Operation "Overlord" would begin.

General Eisenhower with parachute infantry of 101 Airborne Division, a few hours before the start of Operation "Overlord," in the early evening of 5 June. (Note that an overzealous censor has obscured the "Screaming Eagle" divisional formation flashes in this picture.) It was an anxious time for Eisenhower, who had drafted a brief press statement should the "Overlord" landing fail. (IWM photograph EA25491)

A dramatic, and very obviously posed, photograph of British pathfinders of 6 Airborne Division synchronizing watches prior to takeoff, about 2300 hours, 5 June, with the engine of a DC-3 Dakota behind them. Pathfinders were responsible, once on the ground, for marking out the landing sites for the remainder of the division. These four men, Lieutenant Bobby de Latour, Lieutenant Don Wells, Lieutenant John Vischer and Lieutenant Bob Midwood, may have been the first Allied troops to land in Normandy. (IWM photograph H39070)

THE BATTLE OF NORMANDY

The Allied Landings, 6 to 7 June

The Battle of Normandy began at a few minutes after midnight on 6 June 1944 (British double summer time, corresponding to German summer time or GMT plus two hours) as pathfinder paratroops of the three Allied airborne divisions jumped from the transport aircraft that had carried them across the French coast. On landing, these men marked out the drop zones for the approaching paratroop battalions, which would secure the flanks of the Allied amphibious lodgement area. An hour later, men of the American 101 Airborne Division and 82 Airborne Division jumped from their aircraft over the Cotentin Peninsula to secure the exits from the western-

most American beach. Meanwhile paratroops of the British 6 Airborne Division dropped on the eastern flank to capture the crossings over the Orne River and the Canal de Caen. The crucial "Pegasus Bridge" over the canal and the Orne had already been captured by a special glider-borne force from 6 Airborne Division that had come in with the pathfinders. Most of the glider-borne troops of the three divisions would fly in to join the men on the ground later that morning. Despite the fears of heavy casualties, this use of airborne troops was a considerable success. But, dropping by night over uncertain country, some of the American parachute battalions were so badly scattered that they took days to re-form. This experience so impressed their commanders that

British Hamilcar gliders of 6 Airborne Division bringing in the second wave of the division on D-Day, about 1000 hours, 6 June. Each of the airborne divisions had two parachute regiments or brigades and one carried in gliders, which also brought in most of the division's equipment. Although made up of specially picked and trained troops, airborne divisions were inevitably lacking in heavy weapons and artillery pieces, and were vulnerable to tanks. (IWM photograph B5198)

The British battleship HMS Rodney *firing her 16in guns in support of the D-Day landings, 6 June. The other battleships involved in the bombardment were HMS* Nelson, *HMS* Warspite, *HMS* Ramillies, *USS* Texas, *USS* Nevada *and USS* Arkansas. *(IWM photograph A23976)*

Men of 4 U.S. Division on "Utah" Beach, D-Day, 6 June. Although there have been some casualties, it is safe to stand up by full daylight. Note the guard in the background watching for German snipers. The doctor in the foreground has spread out his medical kit and is attending to the wounded. (IWM photograph AT26063)

Men of 16 RCT, 1 U.S. Division, coming ashore at "Omaha" Beach, 0630 hours, 6 June. Note the high tide covering some of the German beach defenses and the "Tankdozer" of Number 10 Engineer Assault Team. 16 RCT should have been supported by 741 Tank Battalion, but only five out of 32 of its amphibious Shermans made it to the shore against the bad weather conditions and German fire. The line of the "Omaha" bluff can be seen in the distance. (IWM photograph AP25726)

for the remainder of the war all further Allied airborne operations were conducted in daylight. Operation "Overlord" began with the first and last major parachute night drop in history.

At 0300 hours, just under two hours after the arrival of the paratroops, nearly two thousand Allied heavy and medium bombers began a two-hour preliminary bombing of the German defenses in the landing area, followed by a bombardment from some seven battleships, 18 cruisers, 43 destroyers, 2 gunboats and a heavy-gun monitor, which had arrived with the invasion fleet off the Normandy coast. Fifteen minutes before the landing craft from the fleet reached the beaches, there was a further attack by a thousand American heavy bombers on the German main line of resistance. The Americans had decided to land an hour earlier than the British to take advantage of a lower tide and fewer submerged obstacles, so reducing their initial naval bombardment to about forty minutes. At 0630 hours, supported by final covering fire from rocket-firing assault craft, the first American troops began to land.

The initial landing forces of 21st Army Group comprised eight specially tailored brigade groups or regimental combat teams, three American, three British and two Canadian. The plan called for First U.S. Army to land on two beaches. The westernmost, code-named "Utah" Beach, was at the base of the Cotentin Peninsula and led directly onto a flat, marshy plain virtually devoid of cover, and deliberately flooded by the Germans as part of their defenses. The two American airborne divisions were in the process of securing the exits inland from "Utah" Beach, and ensuring that the Germans could not use the bridges and causeways through this marsh as choke points. The first unit ashore on "Utah" Beach was 8 RCT of 4 Division, the leading division of VII U.S. Corps, followed by the rest of the division, units of U.S. Rangers, and elements of 90 Division in support. Eastward, a gap of some ten miles (fifteen kilometers) across the estuaries of the Taut and Vire Rivers separated "Utah" Beach from the next landing beach. This was "Omaha" Beach, which was assaulted by 116 RCT of 29 Division and 16 RCT of 1 Division (the famous "Big Red One" division) both part of V U.S. Corps. Between the two beaches, to the

east of the Vire estuary, U.S. 2 and 5 Ranger Battalions carried out an assault on the cliffs at Pointe du Hoc to silence a German coastal battery – which turned out to have no guns in place.

The decision to attack in bad weather presented the troops in the landing craft with serious problems. Tides were running higher, and submerged obstacles were more of a threat, than had been expected. Many of the landing craft were swamped in the approach to the beaches, or lost to obstacles and enemy fire. On the open sand dunes of "Utah" Beach 4 Division landed and secured its objectives with little trouble. The whole division took fewer than 200 casualties on D-Day, by the end of which it had linked up successfully with 101 Airborne Division. But on "Omaha" Beach, 1 Division and 29 Division lost most of their supporting armor and combat engineers before they reached the shoreline, which was dominated by German positions on a high bluff. Unexpectedly, the Americans found themselves facing not only 726 Grenadier Regiment of 716 Static Division, which they had believed to be the only German

German prisoners from 716 Static Division on "Omaha" Beach awaiting shipment back to England, either 6 or 7 June. The mixture of young boys and old men is typical of German static divisions at this date, held together only by fierce and sometimes violent discipline. Some of the prisoners appear to have been given nonregulation boots and may be from an Ost battalion. (IWM photograph PL28213)

division defending the main Allied lodgement area, but also 914 Regiment and 916 Regiment of 352 Division, a veteran formation that had been assigned to the defense of Normandy in January 1944 but had been missed by Allied intelligence. These men, who had survived the initial bombardment relatively unscathed, kept the landing forces pinned down on "Omaha" Beach until the early afternoon of D-Day before giving ground. By the end of the day at "Omaha" the Americans were nowhere more than 2,000 yards inland.

Second British Army began its invasion at 0725 hours. On "Gold" Beach, the westernmost British beach, the assaulting forces were 231 Brigade Group and 69 Brigade Group of 50 (Northumberland) Division, with added armored,

Operation "Overlord," D-Day, 6 June 1944

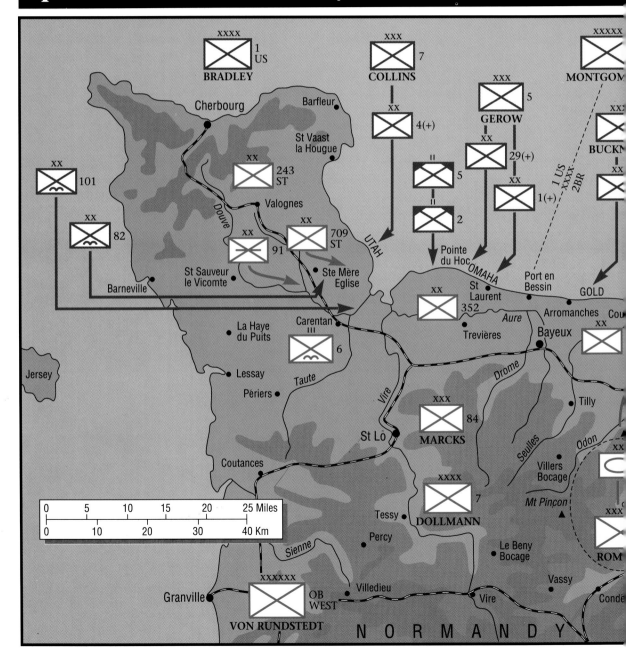

artillery and Commando support as the leading element of XXX British Corps, which made good progress inland against 736 Grenadier Regiment of 716 Static Division. The remaining two beaches both came under I British Corps, although the forces that landed immediately to the east of 50 Division, on "Juno" Beach, were not chiefly British. They were 7 Brigade Group and 8 Brigade Group of 3 Canadian Division, supported by Commandos of 4 Special Service Brigade. The landing at "Juno" Beach was deliberately delayed by ten minutes owing to an offshore shoal, but was successful after hard fighting against 736 Grenadier Regiment and its supporting troops. (In a manner typical of German static divisions, 716 Static Division had two German infantry regiments of two battalions plus two attached Ost infantry battalions.) By early afternoon both 50 Division and 3 Canadian Division were established ashore, with the leading elements of 7 Armored Division ("The Desert Rats") landing later in the day. All their major D-Day objectives were achieved on 6 June or the day following. Under the force of the Allied attack the six battalions of 716 Static Division were reduced to one weak battalion and a combined battle group of fewer than 300 men.

The biggest setback of D-Day for the Allies occurred on the easternmost beach, "Sword" next to the mouth of the Orne River, on which the first troops to land were 8 Brigade Group of 3 British

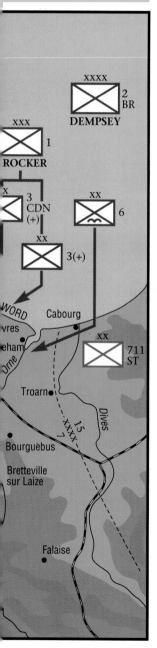

Landing craft of 3 British Division at "Sword" Beach on D-Day, 6 June. The aerial photograph shows the extreme narrowness of the beach due to the unusually high tide, in places no more than 15 yards from the water's edge to the seafront. The intensity of the Allied bombardment can still be seen from the smoking buildings. In places, the trip by landing craft from ship to shore took as long as three hours. (IWM photograph CL25)

"Sword" Beach on D-Day, commandos in the first wave, about 0750 hours, 6 June. Brigadier Lord Lovat, to the right of his men, strides out through the water toward the strong point of La Breche a little to the east of the first Sword landings. Lovat commanded 1 Special Service Brigade (referred to by the British, confusingly, as SS troops). In the foreground, with his back to the camera, is Piper Bill Millin, Lovat's brigade bagpiper, whose pipes are just visible. (IWM photograph B5103)

Signal Troop of Number 6 Commando, part of 1 Special Service Brigade, coming ashore on D-Day, 6 June. These Commandos have all opted to wear their green berets rather than steel helmets. Note the formation badge of Combined Operations on the upper arm. In the background can be seen a bridgelaying tank of 79 Armored Division. The sergeant, carrying a Thompson submachine gun, is identified as Sergeant B. Mapham. Although meant to be a fast moving force, the men are considerably weighed down with equipment and stores. (IWM photograph B5071)

Men of Number 4 Troop, 6 Commando, 1 Special Service Brigade, link up with the men of 6 Airborne Division at Pegasus Bridge. The capture of the bridge was one of the outstanding small-unit actions of the Battle of Normandy. It secured the British flank, preventing the tanks of 21 Panzer crossing the Canal de Caen and Orne River, and it gave 3 British Division an exit into the open country to the east of the city. Note that both the paratroopers are carrying Sten submachine guns with plenty of spare magazines. (IWM photograph B5058)

Division, supported by the Commandos of 1 Special Service Brigade. The initial planning called for 3 Division to advance far enough inland on D-Day to capture the city of Caen, a distance of some ten miles (fifteen kilometers). The high tides resulting from the bad weather, coupled with stiff German resistance, delayed the division's advance and prevented much of its supporting armor getting ashore in time to help. Although it linked up successfully with 6 Airborne Division, 3 Division was confronted north of Caen not only by troops from 716 Static Division but also by tanks and infantry of 21 Panzer Division, part of Rommel's Army Group B reserve. Allied intelligence knew this division to be in the Normandy area but had not expected it to be so close to Caen itself. Much was later made of the failure of 3 Division to break through the German armor and capture Caen, but it is unlikely that the city could have been held even if it had been taken. In the event, neither side got the result it wanted. Although it was able to stop the British drive on Caen, 21 Panzer Division was unable to exploit the gap between "Sword" and "Juno" Beaches, which was closed on 7 June as 3 British Division linked up with 3 Canadian

Division, and the chance for the decisive counterstroke that Rommel had believed crucial was lost. The stalemate in front of Caen which resulted was to dominate the battle of Normandy for the next two months.

The German response to the Allied landing was confused and badly coordinated, an inevitable product of their command system. Generalfeldmarschall Rommel demonstrated his famous ability (seen both at the start of Operation "Crusader" in December 1941 and at El Alamein) for not being there at the crucial time. On 4 June he had gone home to Swabia for his wife's birthday, leaving his chief of staff to look after Army Group B. Generaloberst Dollmann, commanding Seventh Army, was also away from his headquarters, attending a practice wargame in Rennes, while Obergruppenführer "Sepp" Dietrich, commanding I SS Panzer Corps (12 SS Panzer Division and "Panzer Lehr" Division), was in Brussels. All of them hurried back to their commands. In the early hours of D-Day, before the first Allied ground troops were ashore, Generalfeldmarschall von Rundstedt at OB West responded to reports of the invasion by ordering both of Dietrich's divisions

German defenders:
736 Regiment of 716 Static Division

Allied supporting fire
from ships out at sea

Allied air support

Pillboxes and strongpoints

Barbed wire entanglements
and infantry positions

German "hedgehogs" – beach defenses
based on antitank obstacles and mines

Underwater obstacles

A

D-DAY

The landing of British 8 Brigade Group at "Sword" Beach, 0730 hours, 6 June 1944

Each of the landing beaches was divided into smaller beach segments. The first landings at "Sword" were made on "Queen" Beach at the small holiday resort of La Brèche

"Roger" Beach

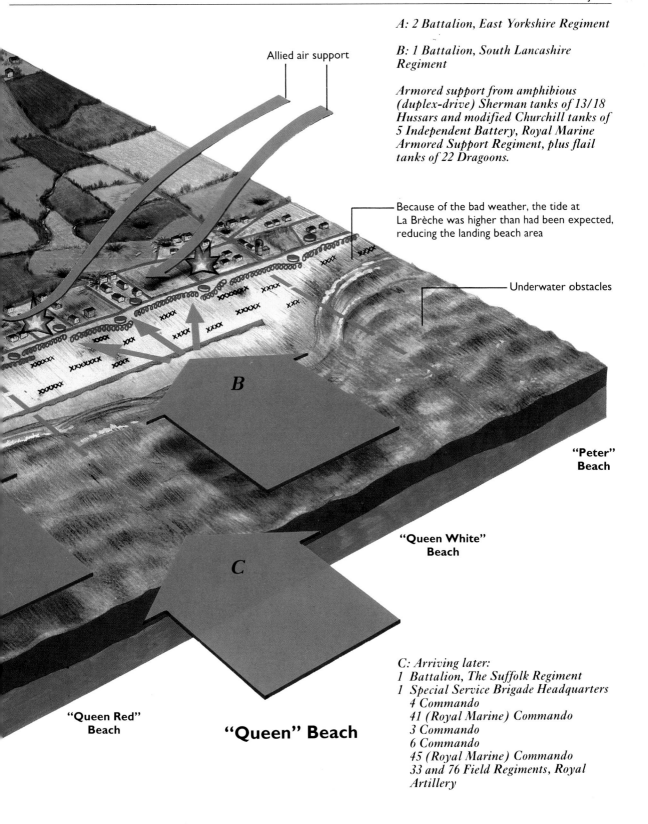

A: 2 Battalion, East Yorkshire Regiment

B: 1 Battalion, South Lancashire Regiment

Armored support from amphibious (duplex-drive) Sherman tanks of 13/18 Hussars and modified Churchill tanks of 5 Independent Battery, Royal Marine Armored Support Regiment, plus flail tanks of 22 Dragoons.

Allied air support

Because of the bad weather, the tide at La Brèche was higher than had been expected, reducing the landing beach area

Underwater obstacles

"Peter" Beach

"Queen White" Beach

B

C

"Queen Red" Beach

"Queen" Beach

C: Arriving later:
1 Battalion, The Suffolk Regiment
1 Special Service Brigade Headquarters
* 4 Commando*
* 41 (Royal Marine) Commando*
* 3 Commando*
* 6 Commando*
* 45 (Royal Marine) Commando*
* 33 and 76 Field Regiments, Royal Artillery*

to move toward the Normandy beaches, and then sought confirmation for the order from OKW. This was not immediately forthcoming, and the divisions waited until Hitler finally approved the order at 1600 hours. Although this delay was much criticized by the German commanders, it probably had no effect on the course of the battle, since to move at all caused the two divisions, like all the German forces moving toward Normandy, serious losses and delays from Allied air attacks. "Panzer Lehr" lost five tanks, 84 armored vehicles and 130 soft-skinned vehicles in its 90 mile (140 kilometer) drive from Lisieux to Caen.

With the invasion confirmed, Geyr von Schweppenburg's Panzer Group West became operational on D-Day and on the following day took over command of the front from the Vire River to the Orne River from Seventh Army. But even Panzer Group West's headquarters lost three-quarters of its radio equipment to air attacks in its journey from Paris to Normandy and could not function properly until 9 June. Two days later, pinpointed by "Ultra" decrypts of its radio traffic, it was hit by a major RAF raid. Geyr von Schweppenburg was wounded and most of his senior officers killed, putting his headquarters out of action for fourteen days and forcing a planned counterattack against the British to be canceled.

This was to be typical of the German experience of Allied air power in Normandy. The ability of Allied ground commanders to call on the waiting "cab ranks" of tactical aircraft, and the damage done by interdiction attacks to German forces long before they reached Normandy, were to be crucial in the winning of the battle. The first counterattack put in by 12 SS Panzer Division against 3 Canadian Division on 7 June, although sufficiently powerful to force the Canadians onto the defensive, was made by only a third of the "Hitler Jugend" Division's troops, the rest being still held up on the road. Between 6 June and 31 August 1944 a total of 480,317 sorties were flown by Allied air forces in support of the troops in Normandy. Nearly half of these were flown by Second Tactical Air Force and U.S. Ninth Air Force, which between them averaged more than 3,000 sorties a day. In contrast, Luftflotte 3 could average only 300 sorties a day at most, and days

went by without German troops even seeing a friendly aircraft. On 17 July, 10 SS Panzer Division recorded its "great joy" that a rare Luftwaffe raid had silenced the Allied artillery on its front for twenty minutes. There was no significant Luftwaffe interference in the D-Day landings, and the Allies continued to enjoy virtual air supremacy over Normandy throughout the battle.

Securing the Beachhead, 7 to 17 June

Although the Allies had not been repulsed on D-Day itself, Rommel continued his strategy of holding them to their initial landing area by a static defense, yielding as little ground as possible. This had the double advantage of reducing the effect of Allied air power, which was just as powerful as he had feared, and of leaving open the possibility of an armored counterstroke down onto the beaches. What little discretion Rommel had in this matter was actually removed by a directive from Hitler on 11 June forbidding any withdrawal at all.

The battlefield of Normandy greatly favored this type of static defense. Except for the flat, marshy areas near the river estuaries at Carentan and Cabourg on either flank of the invasion area, inland from the beaches the countryside of Normandy west of Caen and across the Cotentin Peninsula was characterized by enclosed farmland, a patchwork of small fields bounded by earth banks and overgrown hedgerows, linked by narrow sunken lanes and dotted with small villages and farmhouses often built for defense in medieval times. The checkerboard appearance of the hedgerows, which stretched up to 50 miles (80km) inland from the coast, provided their local name of "bocage" or box-country. This bocage greatly restricted visibility, making armor very hard to deploy and control and very vulnerable to attack at short range by Bazooka or Panzerfaust. Coordination of firepower was hampered as forward observers for artillery or air strikes often had little idea of where they themselves were. (At least one Royal Artillery observer solved this problem by calling down fire on what he believed to be his own position and watching where the shells actually fell.) Above all, fighting in bocage used up combat infantry at an alarming rate. For the

While the Germans hesitated, the Allies landed their first divisions. This is 2 Battalion, Middlesex Regiment, the machine gun battalion of 3 British Division, coming ashore with the second wave in support of 1 Battalion, South Lancashire Regiment, at "Sword" Beach at 0745 on D-Day. Every British division had an extra machine gun battalion equipped with Vickers medium machine guns. Note that the beach is still under fire. (IWM photograph B5114)

The landing area of the British 6 Airborne Division at Ranville, near Caen, with the start of the bocage country clearly visible in the distance. Despite appearances, many of the gliders are not wrecked but were designed to have their fuselages separate for ease of unloading. The bocage in this part of the battlefield, near Caen, was almost open ground compared with the dense country that the Americans were fighting in toward St. Lô. (IWM photograph MH2076)

M4, 3rd Platoon, "B" Company, 8th Tank Battalion, U.S. 4th Armored Division, Avranches. Illustration by Steven J. Zaloga.

British, it was like fighting in the trenches of the Western Front; for some Americans it was like fighting in the jungles of the Pacific. Troops trained in England for open, mobile warfare had to rethink their tactics rapidly.

About 20 miles (30km) south of Bayeux the bocage becomes broken into thickly wooded ridges and cliffs, which stretch south for a further 30 miles (50km), called locally the Suisse Normande from a fancied resemblance to Switzerland. The key feature in this area is Mont Pinçon, a hill some 1,200 feet (400 meters) high lying 20 miles (30km) to the southwest of Caen. On the Vire River at the northern edge of the Suisse Normande is the small country town of St. Lô, the capture of which was vital to American control of the road net in western Normandy.

The only city in the "Overlord" landing area was Caen itself, the regional capital with perhaps 50,000 inhabitants in 1944. About five miles (eight km) southwest of Caen the ground rises gently up to Hill 112 (meters), a little hill that completely dominates the surrounding area, making unob-

served movement very difficult. The high chimneys of Colombelles steelworks less than two miles (three km) to the east of Caen provided the other major observation point in the area. But to the immediate south and southeast of Caen the country stretches away as far south as Falaise in a series of open ridges broken only by small villages and farmhouses. Bourgébus Ridge, three miles (five km) southeast of Caen, dominates the city. It was here that Rommel concentrated his armor, partly to defend against a breakout by the British toward Paris, and partly because the good tank country gave him the best chance of a successful armored counterstroke.

By dusk on 7 June, however, the possibility of the Allies being trapped on the beaches and driven back into the sea was fast receding. Of 156,000 troops landed by sea and air on D-Day about 10,000 had become casualties, a low figure for such an operation. Early on 7 June, Montgomery came ashore and set up 21st Army Group's tactical headquarters. Eisenhower and SHAEF headquarters remained behind in southern England.

The crisis at "Omaha" Beach was past, and the Americans had linked up with the British advancing from "Gold" Beach. By the end of the day all three of the British beaches had also linked into a continuous front, and the town of Bayeux had been liberated. But not all the Allied objectives had been achieved. In particular, against resistance from 21 Panzer Division and 12 SS Panzer Division, there was little prospect of capturing Caen. On 7 June, Rommel moved 2 Panzer Division from Army Group B reserve to the British sector, and von Rundstedt obtained Hitler's permission to move two more divisions, perhaps the most formidable in the German order of battle, toward Caen: 1 SS Panzer Division "Leibstandarte Adolf Hitler" from OKW reserve in Belgium and 2 SS Panzer Division "Das Reich" from Army Group G at Toulouse in southern France. The "Das Reich" Division had expected to cover the distance in five days; but owing to sabotage by French Resistance and directed Allied air strikes on information supplied by members of the Special Air Service its journey took seventeen days instead.

The only Allied landing force still not linked into a continuous front by 8 June was VII U.S. Corps on "Utah" Beach. Overall responsibility for the defense of this part of Normandy rested with Seventh Army's LXXXIV Corps. Although 716 Static Division and 352 Division had fared badly under the weight of the main Allied assault, two more of its three divisions stationed in the Cotentin Peninsula, 91 Airlanding Division and 709 Static Division, were able to intervene against the western flank of the American airborne troops on D-Day, with 243 Static Division coming up in support. German forces in the Cotentin, and indeed throughout the battle, suffered considerably in losing their senior commanders to Allied airpower. The commander of 91 Airlanding Division was ambushed and killed by American paratroops while returning to his division from the Rennes wargames on D-Day; General Marcks, the Corps commander, was killed by an Allied fighter-bomber attack on 12 June, and the commander of 243 Static Division by another on 16 June.

A major problem for VII U.S. Corps was the presence of 6 Parachute Regiment (attached to 91 Airlanding Division but functioning as an independent unit) holding the base of the peninsula and the town of Carentan. An offensive by 101 Airborne Division from "Utah" Beach and 29

United States infantryman. Illustration by Mark Iley.

Division from "Omaha" Beach, aimed at linking the two beachheads, began on 7 June. But the American airborne troops, themselves lightly armed, met considerable resistance from 6 Parachute Regiment, and not until the morning of 10 June did patrols from the two divisions link up to form a notionally continuous front.

Rommel regarded the defense of Carentan as crucial to his strategy of pinning the Allies close to the beaches. On 7 June he ordered II Parachute Corps, comprising 3 Parachute Division, 77 Division and 275 Division, to move from Brittany to the west of the Cotentin, so prolonging and reinforcing the line of LXXXIV Corps. With them was dispatched from OKW reserve the only German élite division not directed toward the defense of Caen, 17 SS Panzergrenadier Division. Again, Allied air attacks and French Resistance sabotage delayed the arrival of this division, its leading elements not reaching their positions southwest of Carentan until dusk on 11 June. That night, in another rare appearance by the Luftwaffe, eighteen tons of ammunition were airdropped to 6 Parachute Regiment in Carentan. It was not enough. A nightlong attack by 101 Airborne Division, supported by massive firepower from artillery and naval gunnery, captured the town by dawn on 12 June. An attempted counterattack by 17 SS Panzergrenadier Division later that morning was repulsed as more American troops arrived from "Utah" Beach. The Allied line inland from the beaches was now both continuous and secure.

Meanwhile, V U.S. Corps had driven inland from "Omaha" Beach on 12 June, heading for St. Lô. On 12 June XIX U.S. Corps was activated, and three days later VIII U.S. Corps, but First U.S. Army under Bradley was still not strong enough to overcome German opposition in the bocage. A sustained push by 29 Division, begun on 15 June, penetrated to within five miles (eight km) of St. Lô in three days' fighting before being halted.

While the Americans were expanding the beachhead, Second British Army under General Dempsey was searching for a soft spot in the German defenses of Caen. An attempt was made by XXX British Corps to exploit the gap between 352 Division, being driven back from "Omaha"

by U.S. 1 Division, and "Panzer Lehr" Division, the westernmost of the armored divisions defending Caen. On 12 June a good start was made as XXX Corps's leading formation, 7 Armored Division, drove past Panzer Lehr's western flank and into the gap, reaching the vital road junction at Villers Bocage, about fifteen miles (25km) southwest of Caen, early next morning. The leading tanks of 7 Armored were then attacked in turn by Tiger tanks of 501 SS Heavy Tank Battalion (part of I SS Panzer Corps reserve), by 2 Panzer Division arriving from the south, and by "Panzer Lehr" Division from the east. In a celebrated action at Villers Bocage itself, the leading British regiment lost twenty of its Cromwell tanks to an attack by five Tigers led by Obersturmführer Michael Wittmann, whose own tank knocked out at least ten Cromwells in five minutes. On 14 June a frontal attack by 50 Division against "Panzer Lehr," attempting to reach 7 Armored, ended in failure, and only supporting artillery fire from 1 U.S. Division prevented the British armored division, trapped between 2 Panzer and "Panzer Lehr," being driven back. That night 7 Armored withdrew about five miles (eight km) from Villers Bocage to a more secure position.

The extremely controversial episode of Villers Bocage lost Second British Army its best chance of capturing Caen that month. Together with the American failure to capture St. Lô, it brought the Allied advance to a temporary halt. The one Allied success was the attack by "Lightning Joe" Collins's VII U.S. Corps on 14 July westward across the Cotentin Peninsula. Led by 9 Division and 82 Airborne Division, this drive reached the west coast of the Cotentin at Barneville on 17 June, cutting off 243 Static Division, 77 Division and 709 Static Division in the northern part of the peninsula. Hitler, overruling Rommel, ordered these divisions to hold in place rather than retreating southward or falling back on Cherbourg, resulting in their complete destruction by the end of the month as VII Corps fought its way up the peninsula. Meanwhile, VII U.S. Corps under Troy Middleton, which had been intended as part of Third U.S. Army, took over the Cotentin front facing south.

The Break-In, 18 to 24 Junej56

The success of VII U.S. Corps enabled 21st Army Group for the first time to present a single face southward toward the enemy. In broad terms, on the eastern flank near Caen, Second British Army with two armored, five infantry and one airborne division faced Panzer Group West with four armored and one static division (plus one static division of LXXXI Corps, which was just in Fifteenth Army area east of the Orne). On the western flank, First U.S. Army with one armored, eight infantry and two airborne divisions faced Seventh Army with one mechanized division, six infantry divisions, one parachute, one airlanding and one static division. In round numbers of divisions the Americans had a small advantage over the Germans. The British had a slightly larger advantage, offset by the German assembly of armored divisions.

The Allied numerical superiority was not yet great enough for a decisive breakout, but if things were not running perfectly for Montgomery, he was undoubtedly winning the battle. By 17 June there were 557,000 Allied troops, 81,000 vehicles and 183,000 tons of supplies ashore. The number of troops landing each day exceeded the number of casualty replacements required, and although there were local difficulties there was never a serious shortage of fuel, ammunition or supplies. The German forces, on the other hand, were paying dearly in order to hold the ground so close to the beaches. The infantry regiments of both Seventh Army and Panzer Group West were taking casualties at a far greater rate than they were being replaced, and as the infantry dwindled the tanks of the armored divisions were being sucked into the front line to act as armored pillboxes. Progressively, Rommel's divisions were being reduced to battle group size by Allied artillery, air power, and even the guns of the warships out at sea. By the third week of June, I SS Panzer Corps ("Panzer Lehr," 12 SS Panzer, 21 Panzer, 716 Static Division and 101 SS Heavy Tank Battalion) had only 129 Panzer IVs and 46 Panthers as runners, every one of its 30 Tiger tanks being in need of repair. The battalions of 346 Static Division, on the far right of the German line, were down to between 140 and 240 men in strength, and three of the infantry divisions facing the Americans had suffered similar losses. Army Group B as a whole had lost over 26,000 casualties, including an army corps commander and five divisional commanders dead. Some British and American units suffered just as heavily in the fight. The lightly equipped 82 U.S. Airborne Division lost 1,259 men on D-Day alone and took 46 percent casualties before being relieved in early July. The difference was that the Allies were able to withdraw divisions and replace their losses. The Germans could do neither.

Allied attacks were also draining away Army Group B's reserves of supplies, fuel and ammunition as air interdiction now paralyzed 90 percent of the rail network in the Normandy area and harassed road transport. The German armored divisions arrived in Normandy weakened and delayed not only from direct air attacks but from halts imposed by fuel shortages. For the first ten days of the battle Seventh Army received from Army Group B only a quarter of the fuel and three-fifths of the ammunition that it needed, and had to make up the rest from local stocks.

On 16 June, Adolf Hitler issued a new directive intended to provide reinforcements for Normandy without weakening Fifteenth Army, still waiting to repel the nonexistent FUSAG. To 1 SS Panzer Division and 2 SS Panzer Division, already in transit for Normandy, he added II SS Panzer Corps (9 SS Panzer and 10 SS Panzer) from the Eastern Front. From First Army in southwest France, LXXXVI Corps (with two divisions) was ordered northward. In addition, "Panzer Lehr," 2 Panzer and 12 SS Panzer would be withdrawn into reserve and their places taken by infantry divisions from Fifteenth Army and Nineteenth Army. Troops from Scandinavia would replace the divisions moved from Fifteenth Army, which would end up stronger than before. This would free a total of seven armored divisions for a counterattack in Normandy. Meanwhile, all troops would hold their present positions.

From Hitler's command post at Rastenburg this appeared a reasonable plan. But from the experience of the previous two weeks Rommel and von Rundstedt were aware that any divisions sent

North American P-51B-5-NT Mustang, 43-24823, of 362nd Fighter Squadron, 357th Fighter Group, 66th Fighter Wing, VIII Fighter Command, U.S. 8th Air Force. Illustration by Michael Roffe.

The partially completed British Mulberry harbor at Arromanches on 12 June 1944. The blockships or "Gooseberries" have been sunk out in the bay to form a breakwater and the large jetties or "Whales" positioned to form the outer harbor. The floating piers are being built out from the shore to reach the jetties. As a piece of engineering, nothing like this had ever been attempted before. (IWM photograph B5717)

The results of "The Great Storm." This is part of the wreckage of the American Mulberry at St. Laurent, taken on 24 June. As a result of the storm the Americans gave up constructing their Mulberry but continued to offload their ships' cargoes onto landing craft in the lee of the Gooseberry blockships. (IWM photograph B6100)

to Normandy would arrive understrength, late, with insufficient supplies, and would rapidly be decimated by Allied firepower. In response to their disquiet, Hitler himself flew out to meet them near Soissons on 17 June, only to turn down their requests for more local control over their own forces and the authority to order retreats as necessary. He then flew the 600 miles (950km) back to Rastenburg without ever seeing the Normandy battlefield and continued to direct the daily conduct of the battle from his maps. In contrast, although Eisenhower visited Montgomery, Bradley and Dempsey at their headquarters several times during the battle, he made no attempt to interfere with its running. Winston Churchill visited the beachhead once, as an observer, on 12 June.

Until 12th Army Group was activated, and Eisenhower took over control of the ground battle from Montgomery, there was little for the SHAEF staff to do except watch the battle and worry. Air Chief Marshal Tedder, as Eisenhower's deputy and the senior airman at SHAEF, felt the failure to take Caen and deliver the Caen-Falaise plain as bases for his aircraft very strongly. There was deployment space for only one fighter-bomber group, 83 Group of Second Tactical Air Force, in Normandy, with the rest of Leigh-Mallory's forces left stuck in southern England. On 13 June the first V-1 flying bombs began to fall on London and the south of England from launching sites in the Pas de Calais area, making it even more urgent for the British to advance and bring these sites within range of their air and ground forces in France. In addition, the whole Allied plan for victory depended on their buildup being faster than that of the Germans. Because of the failure of the D-Day landings to go exactly as planned, the landing schedule was running two days late, the equivalent of three American RCTs and two British armored brigade groups. Together with the failure to capture Caen, this was sufficient for Tedder and Coningham to inform their air commanders on 14 June that the situation had the makings of a dangerous crisis. Even Montgomery considered that the tempo of operations had slowed, and he was eager to quicken it again.

With Cherbourg not yet captured, all the

Allied supplies were landing over the beaches and through the partially completed Mulberry harbors, St. Laurent for First U.S. Army and Arromanches for Second British Army. On 19 June the generally bad weather broke into a severe gale that raged for four days in the English Channel, considerably damaging the two Mulberries, and running at least 700 ships and small craft aground. The daily rate at which the Allies could land dropped by roughly two-thirds, from 34,712 to 9,847 men a day, 5,894 to 2,426 vehicles a day, and 24,974 tons to 7,350 tons of stores a day. The American Mulberry was so badly damaged that it was abandoned altogether, and it was not until the end of the month that landings from the British Mulberry and across the beaches were once more taking place at the planned rate.

The four days of "The Great Storm" (as the British called the gale) threw the Allied landing timetable out by six divisions, or about a week. This partly accounts for the week's delay in the Allied breakout a month later, in which time they almost convinced themselves that they had lost the battle. During the gale, Allied aircraft were grounded, and no offensive could be mounted. This, if at any time, was the moment for a German counterattack. On 20 June OKW headquarters ordered von Rundstedt to prepare plans for six armored divisions to attack on the boundary between the British and Americans and drive through to Bayeux. Of the divisions named, three had not yet arrived and two were still holding the line at Caen. All that Rommel and von Rundstedt could do was wait for the next Allied attack. By this time most of the German higher commanders were convinced that they were fighting a hopeless battle, and indeed a hopeless war.

The Breakthrough, 25 June to 10 July

On 18 June Montgomery had issued a directive calling for the capture of Cherbourg by the Americans and Caen by the British before 23 June. The bad weather delayed both operations. On the American flank the fortress of Cherbourg surrendered to VII Corps on 26 June and the port on the following day, but it was not until 1 July that all resistance in the peninsula ceased. Cherbourg was expected to discharge 150,000 tons within four weeks, but it had been so thoroughly sabotaged by the Germans that it was not to reach full capacity until the end of September.

The British offensive was another attempt to outflank Caen from the west, where XLVII Panzer Corps now commanded the remaining battle groups of 2 Panzer and "Panzer Lehr." Codenamed Operation "Epsom," its intention was for Lieutenant General O'Connor's VIII Corps to break through between "Panzer Lehr" and 12 SS Panzer, the westernmost division of I SS Panzer Corps defending Caen itself. O'Connor's force would then swing eastward through the bocage, across the Odon River, and capture Hill 112. On 25 June, Operation "Dauntless," a subsidiary attack by XXX Corps, secured the western flank of VIII Corps's advance, which began on the following day. After a bombardment by over 700 guns, O'Connor's leading unit, 15 (Scottish) Division, broke through the defenses of 12 SS Panzer, with 11 Armored Division following up. In the bocage, VIII Corps made progress at slightly more than 2,000 yards a day. Bad weather prevented any flying from southern England and limited the support from 83 Group in Normandy. But on 29 June, the day after 1 SS Panzer had arrived to reinforce 12 SS Panzer, 11 Armored Division pushed forward to the northern slopes of Hill 112.

In response, Generaloberst Dollmann of Seventh Army was forced to give up the newly arrived II SS Panzer Corps and commit it against the British. Coming into line between XLVII Panzer Corps and I SS Panzer Corps late on 29 June, the two fresh Waffen-SS armored divisions threatened O'Connor's southern flank. That night, after consulting Dempsey, O'Connor pulled 11 Armored back from Hill 112 and went onto the defensive. In fact, badly mauled by Allied air attacks in the improving weather, II SS Panzer Corps could not start its counterattack until 1 July and made no headway in the bocage, leaving the British with the ground won during "Epsom." At the cost of some 4,000 casualties. VIII Corps had achieved a penetration only five miles (eight km) deep and two miles (three km) wide. But its attack had pulled a further two German armored divisions into the defense of Caen, and placed the city in an untenable salient.

By 30 June the Allies had landed in Normandy 875,000 men, 150,000 vehicles and 570,000 tons of stores. Second British Army had ashore three armored, ten infantry divisions and one airborne division, while First U.S. Army mustered two armored, nine infantry and two airborne divisions. Of these, four British and five American divisions had been fighting since D-Day. The Americans had taken 37,034 casualties and the British 24,698 casualties, receiving between them 79,000 replacements. The Germans, in response, had committed to the battle about 400,000 men, leaving a further 250,000 in Fifteenth Army waiting for the Pas de Calais invasion. By 7 July, Army Group B had taken 80,783 casualties and received about 4,000 replacements. Panzer Group West, defending Caen, consisted of seven armored, four infantry divisions and one Luftwaffe field division with altogether 725 tanks. In addition, the multibarreled rocket launchers of three German Werfer brigades and the antitank guns of III Flak Corps had all been concentrated in the British sector. Seventh Army had one mechanized division, three infantry divisions, one airlanding and one parachute division in line, plus 2 SS Panzer Division in reserve – in all, no more than 140 tanks.

Despite this strong position, many Allied commanders were worried about their failure to take more territory. By early July, when they had expected to have liberated Alençon, Rennes and St. Malo, they were nowhere more than fifteen miles (25km) inland, occupying one-fifth of the area anticipated in Montgomery's original plan. Lieutenant General Crerar, commanding First Canadian Army, and Lieutenant General Patton, commanding Third U.S. Army, were both ashore in Normandy. But in the cramped beachhead there was no room to deploy two further armies. So long as 12th Army Group could not be formed, Montgomery continued in command. The Americans had nine further divisions in England and, counting their forces for the planned landing in the south of France, a total of 48 divisions waiting to join the campaign in Europe, thirteen of them armored. The British, in contrast, were running out of troops, particularly infantry. All three of their armored divisions were now in Normandy,

A Churchill tank of 7 Royal Tank Regiment, 31 Tank Brigade, supports an advance by 8 Battalion, Royal Scots Fusiliers, 15 (Scottish) Division, on 28 June during Operation "Epsom." The British distinguished between tank brigades, usually of heavier tanks such as the Churchill, and armored brigades of Shermans. Altogether they had eight armored or tank brigades, the equivalent of two extra armored divisions, in Normandy by the end of the battle, usually attached to infantry divisions for direct support. (IWM photograph B6124)

Men of 2 Battalion, Gordon Highlanders, 15 (Scottish) Division (note the very clear formation sign), waiting to go forward on 27 June during Operation "Epsom." On the right is a Sherman Flail tank of 79 Armored Division with its turret turned toward the rear for flailing. These were used to clear mines in the path of advancing troops. (IWM photograph B6013)

Not a paratroop drop but a resupply to British 6 Airborne Division by RAF Stirling bombers on 23 June. The positions of 6 Airborne at St. Aubin d'Arquenay on the eastern flank of the still very small beachhead were too exposed for supplies to get through easily overland, and the rate of supplies landing over the beaches had still not recovered from The Great Storm. (IWM photograph B5880)

and only six Canadian and British divisions, two of them armored, were left in England. In future, Second British Army would not be able to replace its casualties at the same rate. Montgomery's plan was deliberately pulling the main German forces onto the weaker of his two armies, and the heavy drain on the infantry caused by bocage fighting was about to have a serious effect on Second British Army's conduct of operations.

The Allied airmen, as before, were the least contented. Unable to grasp their own side's weakness in tanks and infantry against the Germans, they criticized Montgomery heavily for failing to launch an all-out offensive. The more assistance they offered them, the more reluctant the ground troops seemed to be to advance. Indeed, in a new

Operation "Overlord," Situation 1 July 1944 (D+24)

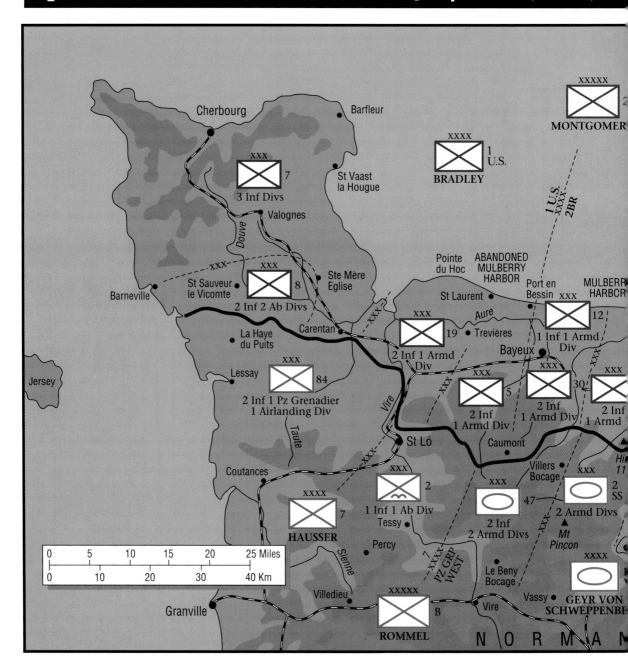

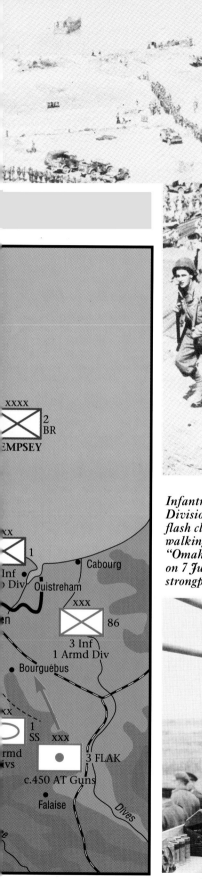

Infantry of 2 U.S. Division, their formation flash clearly visible, walking inland from "Omaha" Beach probably on 7 June, past a German strongpoint that had given considerable trouble on D-Day. Even in one platoon, the mixture of lighter or darker olive-drab uniforms is very noticeable. Although their fighting quality was low at first compared with the best German troops, the American reserves of infantry were crucial to winning the battle. (IWM photograph EA25902)

Squadron Leader J. G. Edison of the Royal Canadian Air Force, as Senior Flying Control Officer, controlling fighter-bombers flying in to land in Normandy for the first time, July 1944. Note the flare pistol and flares on the work-surface of his command truck. Nearly half the squadrons of 83 Group were from the Royal Canadian Air Force. Australian, New Zealand, Polish, Czech, Dutch, French and Norwegian squadrons also fought in Normandy. (IWM photograph CL94)

An RAF or RCAF Typhoon (squadron not identified) takes off from a temporary landing strip in Normandy, early July. Note the four rockets slung under each wing. The black-and-white "invasion stripes" at the wing roots were painted onto all Allied aircraft involved in the Battle of Normandy as a recognition device. Their presence is often a useful check of the authenticity of film or photographs of the battle. (IWM photograph CL147)

The weather in Normandy during the battle alternated from summer heat to torrential rain, forcing both sides to fight in either dust or mud. This picture was taken in VIII British Corps area in the "Epsom" salient on 3 July. Note the sign printed on the jeep's canvas hood warning that, like all American vehicles supplied to the British, it is left-hand drive. (IWM photograph B6321)

A Handley Page Halifax of RAF Bomber Command over Caen during the "Charnwood" bombing of 7 July. Although flares were used in the bombing, it was still quite light at the attack time of 2150 hours (British double summer time). The smoke gives a good idea of the limited aiming accuracy possible for heavy bombers used in this way. (IWM photograph CL347)

directive of 30 June, Montgomery stressed the importance, in drawing the Germans onto Second British Army, of not exposing that army to any setbacks. By 5 July, 83 Group had been joined in Normandy by about half the squadrons of Ninth U.S. Air Force, but the remainder still could not cross the Channel. Tedder and Leigh–Mallory had been promised 27 airfields for their fighter-bombers and only nineteen were operational. Altogether, the buildup was between ten and fifteen squadrons behind schedule. In a beachhead so narrow, finding space to take off and land without coming under German shellfire or risking midair collision was becoming increasingly difficult.

By the first week of July the fear was emerging both at SHAEF and at First U.S. Army headquarters of a possibly stalemated front. Bradley was pessimistic after the slow progress of his renewed drive southward, intended to bring the rest of his forces up level with V Corps in front of St. Lô. The drive had started on 3 July as VIII Corps (including a very weak 82 Airborne Division) advanced down the western coast of the Cotentin Peninsula, with VII Corps joining in a day later and XIX Corps on 7 July, spreading the attack eastward. Through the bocage the Americans made progress at rather less than 2,000 yards a day against the battle groups of LXXXIV Corps, in some cases barely reaching the main German defensive line, and by 11 July the offensive had spent itself. Only Montgomery remained optimistic about the way the battle was going.

Meanwhile, the equally deep mood of pessimism that had afflicted the German higher commanders overcame their sense of obedience. Dramatically, Generaloberst Dollmann of Seventh Army committed suicide on 28 June during Operation "Epsom," being replaced by Obergruppenführer Paul Hausser of II SS Panzer Corps. Rommel was once more away from the front at a crucial moment. He and von Rundstedt were visiting Rastenburg for a further, inconclusive, meeting with Hitler. On their return to France, Geyr von Schweppenburg submitted to von Rundstedt a report, strongly backed by Rommel and Hausser, on the importance of giving up some ground in order to conduct a flexible defense. This von

Rundstedt passed to OKW headquarters with his strong endorsement on 1 July, following it with the somewhat tactless telephone suggestion to make peace at once. On the following day Hitler replaced von Rundstedt at OB West with Generalfeldmarschall Günther von Kluge. Geyr von Schweppenburg's replacement at Panzer Group West a few days later was General Heinrich Eberbach. Obergruppenführer Hausser, over Rommel's objections, was confirmed in command of Seventh Army.

As the American drive ended, Second British Army began its own offensive to capture Caen. Code-named Operation "Charnwood," this revived an earlier idea of Leigh-Mallory's of achieving an advance by carpet bombing the enemy positions with heavy four-engined bombers in direct support of the ground forces, as at Monte Cassino in Italy in February and March that year. With only a few complaints, RAF Bomber Command agreed, and at 2150 hours on 7 July about 460 Lancasters and Halifaxes dropped 2,300 tons of bombs onto the northern outskirts of Caen. Most of these were set with time fuses to explode among the defenders of 12 SS Panzer Division at 0420 on 8 July, just as I British Corps (including 3 Canadian Division) began its attack, supported by artillery, naval gunnery and air strikes. Fighting was fierce. At one point the commander of the "Hitler Jugend" was seen striding through the masonry-filled streets, carrying a Panzerfaust. Of his division only a battalion's worth of infantry and 40 tanks escaped, while 16 Luftwaffe Field Division, defending eastern Caen, took 75 percent casualties. By the morning of 9 July all of Caen north of the Orne River had been cleared. Unfortunately, the aiming points that the Allies had chosen for their heavy bombers had largely missed the German defensive positions. Although the city of Caen and its inhabitants suffered heavily from the bombing, it had little effect on the battle other than to boost the attackers' morale. This partly confirmed the worst opinions of the airmen about their own ground forces. On 10 July, VIII Corps, from its salient west of Caen, launched a new drive code-named Operation "Jupiter," which got back onto the northern slopes of Hill 112 and threatened the western bank of the Orne.

By this time the Germans were doing little but reacting to each Allied blow. They had a choice of three strategies, each of which would lose the battle. They could retreat and concede Normandy to the Allies, but this was forbidden by Hitler, and would give the Allies space to deploy their full ground and air power. Also, it would require the kind of mobile defense that was proving, as Rommel had predicted, impossible to conduct. They could continue to reinforce the Caen sector, leaving their front against the Americans dangerously weak. Or they could reinforce against the Americans, and have the British break out over the good tank country east of Caen. What they could not

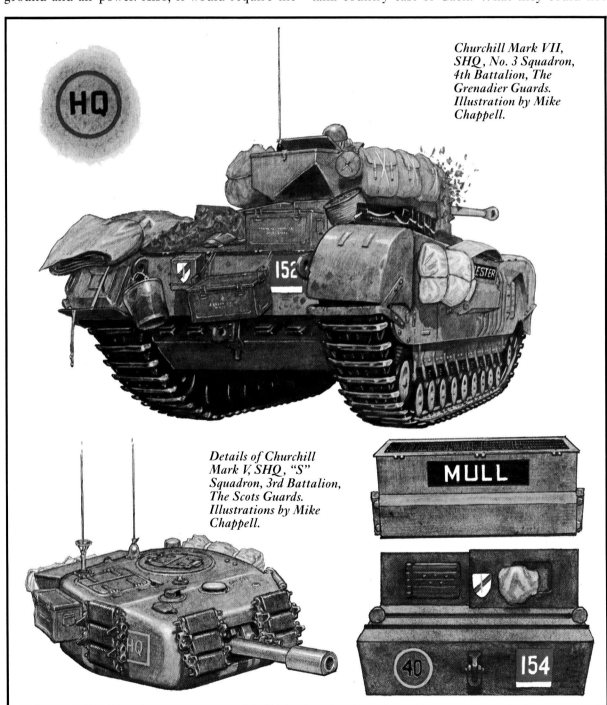

Churchill Mark VII, SHQ, No. 3 Squadron, 4th Battalion, The Grenadier Guards. Illustration by Mike Chappell.

Details of Churchill Mark V, SHQ, "S" Squadron, 3rd Battalion, The Scots Guards. Illustrations by Mike Chappell.

do was create the armored reserve that Hitler wanted. On 5 July, "Panzer Lehr" was finally pulled out of the line to rest, only to be recommitted against XIX U.S. Corps on 11 July. In view of Montgomery's strategy, Bradley was not pleased to find his men facing a German armored division, however weak and tired. When, after "Charnwood," LXXXVI Corps took over the whole sector east of Caen from I SS Panzer Corps, the two armored divisions were deployed south and east of the city against an expected British offensive rather than being grouped in a centralized reserve. Generally, the German formations were so weak that the arriving infantry

The northern part of Caen on 10 July after its capture by the Allies, showing the effects of the bombing and subsequent streetfighting. The Germans made considerable propaganda use of the French civilians hurt or killed in these attacks. (IWM photograph B6912)

A remarkable photograph of men of 1 Battalion, King's Own Scottish Borderers, 3 British Division (note the formation sign), in Caen on 10 July. They have captured from the Germans a Hotchkiss machine gun, seized by the Germans in turn from the French Army in 1940. A substantial amount of German equipment in Normandy was of French origin. (Considering the camera angle, this is probably a posed photograph.) (IWM photograph B6918)

divisions formed a supplement to the armor rather than a replacement for it.

The Breakout, 10 July to 5 August

Montgomery and his two subordinates now planned the decisive phase of the battle, to enable the Americans to break out into Brittany. On 10 July, he issued a directive on how this would be achieved. Bradley would start an offensive toward Avranches, after which VIII Corps, as the spearhead of Third U.S. Army, would swing west into Brittany while First U.S. Army would drive toward Le Mans and Alençon. To aid this, Second British Army would launch a major armored offensive through the open country east of Caen. Bradley's offensive, set to begin on 19 July, was codenamed Operation "Cobra," while Dempsey's, set to begin the day before, was Operation "Goodwood."

First U.S. Army could not break out, however, until the capture of St. Lô, more than a month overdue on the original "Overlord" planning schedule. On 11 July, XIX U.S. Corps changed the direction of its drive southward against II Parachute Corps holding the St. Lô front, only to run into "Panzer Lehr's" counterattack. By weight of

firepower and persistence the Americans pushed the Germans back the four miles (six km) through the rubble of St. Lô, which was secured by the morning of 19 July, too late for the original "Cobra" schedule. The whole offensive, from the start of VIII Corps's attack on 3 July, had cost the Americans 40,000 casualties, 90 percent of them infantrymen. On 20 July torrential rain caused the "Cobra" offensive to be postponed until 24 July.

But if the Americans were in no condition to attack, the Germans were certainly in no condition to defend. By the middle of July, Army Group B had lost nearly 96,400 men and received 5,200 replacements. it had lost 225 tanks and received just seventeen. The entire rifle strength of II Parachute Corps was 3,400 men, including one composite battle group made up from the remains of four infantry divisions. "Panzer Lehr," holding the line just west of St. Lô, numbered 40 tanks and 2,200 men. Both II Parachute Corps and LXXXIV Corps reported to Seventh Army that they were probably too weak to stop another American offensive – information passed at once to the Allies through "Ultra." There was nothing in reserve behind these skeleton formations except four weak battalions of 275 Division. Unless the

A prisoner from 12 SS Panzer Division "Hitler Jugend," captured by men of 59 (Staffordshire) Division in Caen on 8 July, being escorted to the rear by a RASC private of 3 British Division. The youthful appearance of this prisoner gives a correct impression of the "Hitler Jugend" Division. The average age including officers was eighteen and a half years old. The division had never been in action before, but a high proportion of its officers and NCOs had combat experience. (IWM photograph B6596)

Germans could redeploy their forces, they had nothing to stop the next American attack.

Second British Army's offensive, Operation "Goodwood," was the single most controversial episode in the whole Battle of Normandy. British casualties had also reached 40,000 by the middle of July, again mostly infantry. With such a drain on the infantry the celebrated British regimental system was breaking down, for troops were now being assigned to battalions as available and needed. But, because the advance inland had gone neither as far nor as fast as expected, there was a surplus of tanks. To the west, next to First U.S. Army, the line was held by Bucknall's XXX Corps. Next to this, the "Epsom" salient had been taken over by XII Corps and the northern part of Caen by II Canadian Corps, both newly formed, leaving Crocker's I Corps holding the line east of Caen as before. This enabled Montgomery to pull all three of his armored divisions back into reserve under VIII Corps. Montgomery would later say that this ability to create an armored reserve, while the Germans could not, was the moment that he knew the battle was won.

The plan for "Goodwood" called for a subsidiary attack by XXX Corps and XII Corps,

Operation "Greenline," to pin down the German forces in the old "Epsom" salient. Then on 18 July the sector east of Caen would be attacked. The German front was held to a depth of three miles (five km) by battle groups of 16 Luftwaffe Field Division and 21 Panzer Division, supported by III Flak Corps. On the western flank, II Canadian Corps would execute a double envelopment of Caen, finally driving the Germans out of the city and the Colombelles steelworks. On the eastern flank, 3 British Division would attack southeastward to expand the bridgehead. In the center, Allied firepower would be substituted for infantry. A gap 7,000 yards wide would be blown right the way through the German defenses by more than a thousand Allied heavy and medium bombers. The bombing would be followed by a barrage from 750

American firepower. U.S. 987 Artillery Battalion of 105mm self-propelled guns coming ashore at "Omaha" Beach on 7 June. Note in the background the two LSTs (Landing Ship, Tank) which have deliberately beached themselves and opened their bow doors to discharge cargo before floating off again at high tide. This emergency method of unloading was developed in response to the supply problems of D-Day. (IWM photograph B5131)

Panzerkampfwagen V Ausf A, Panther. A command tank, 1.SS-Pz-Div. "Leibstandarte Adolf Hitler." Illustration by David E. Smith.

guns, including naval gunnery, and fighter-bomber attacks. Altogether 4,500 Allied aircraft would be used in the operation. Then, from reserve behind I Corps, across the Canal de Caen and the Orne River, the three armored divisions of VIII Corps would advance on a one-regiment front, one after the other, through the German positions and on to Bourgébus Ridge. The whole operation would involve 250 tanks with the flanking forces and 750 with O'Connor's main punch.

After preliminary planning and discussion with SHAEF, Montgomery issued Lieutenant General Dempsey with a directive on 15 July setting out his aims. The first British objective was to bring the German armor into battle, so that it could not be used against the Americans for the forthcoming Operation "Cobra." The second objective was to secure the remainder of Caen.

O'Connor's tanks were expected to get on to Bourgébus Ridge and his armored car patrols to push on to Falaise, but any further operation would have to wait upon events. "Goodwood" was a typically cautious Montgomery plan. So long as I SS Panzer Corps and II SS Panzer Corps stayed where they were, any result except an outright British retreat was acceptable in terms of his strategy. Montgomery was in the enviable position of being right whatever he did.

Bradley and Dempsey were quite clear on the objectives of "Goodwood." Montgomery's directive, however, never reached SHAEF headquarters. The idea of a massed armored attack, and particularly the mention of Falaise, led Eisenhower and Tedder to believe that here at last was Montgomery's all-out offensive to break out of the beachhead. Montgomery left Eisenhower with the

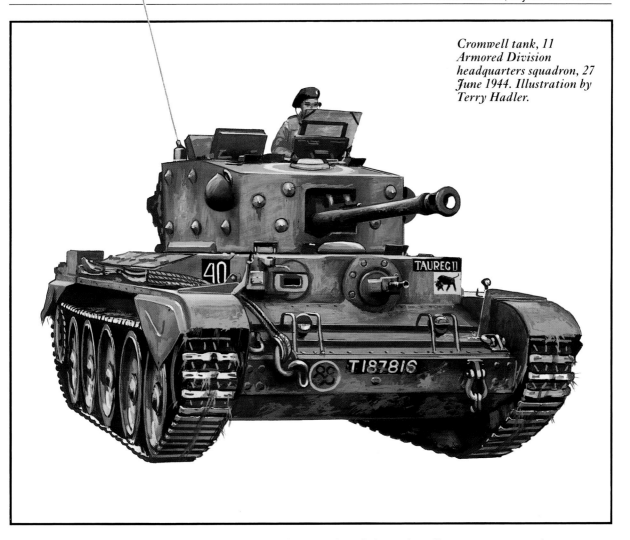

Cromwell tank, 11 Armored Division headquarters squadron, 27 June 1944. Illustration by Terry Hadler.

impression, which he did little to correct, that his strategy was one of double envelopment with "Goodwood" breaking out in the east and "Cobra" in the west, or even that "Cobra" was the subsidiary operation.

On the night of 15 July, Operation "Greenline" began, pinning 2 Panzer, 9 SS Panzer and 10 SS Panzer in position west of Caen, and forcing 1 SS Panzer back into the battle to hold the Orne River. For Operation "Goodwood" the absence of Generalfeldmarschall Rommel from the battlefield at a crucial moment could this time be forgiven. On 17 July his staff car was attacked by a passing Allied fighter-bomber. Rommel was badly wounded and taken to hospital. He was not replaced in command of Army Group B, Generalfeldmarschall von Kluge taking over that appointment in addition to OB West, so finally

rationalizing the German command structure. Three days later, on 20 July, officers of the German Army made the ultimate criticism of Hitler's strategy by attempting to kill him with a bomb in his own headquarters, after which they intended to attempt to negotiate peace with the Allies. The bomb went off, but Hitler was not seriously injured. None of the senior German commanders in Normandy was involved except the convalescent Rommel, who was allowed to commit suicide rather than face trial.

At 0745 on 18 July, after an aerial bombardment of more than two hours' duration, Operation "Goodwood" started. Caen was cleared successfully by II Canadian Corps, and 3 British Division also achieved its objectives. In the center, 11 Armored Division started to move forward, followed by Guards Armored and 7 Armored,

ANTITANK GUNS

	Weight of shell (lb)	Maximum range (yds)	Muzzle velocity (yds/sec)
USA			
57mm towed	6	10,260	2,800
76mm towed	13	10,000	2,700
(also in M18 Hellcat and later models of M4 Sherman)			
3in towed	15	16,100	2,600
(also in M10 Wolverine)			
British			
6pdr towed	6	10,260	2,800
17pdr towed	17	17,000	2,800
(also in Sherman Firefly)			
German			
75mm PaK 40	15	7,680	1,798
88mm PaK 43	23	17,500	2,461

EFFECTIVENESS OF TANK AND ANTITANK GUNS ON ENEMY TANKS

(depth of penetration of armor plate sloped at 30 degrees)

	Range to target in yards			
	100m	500m	1000m	2000m
USA				
75mm (Sherman, Cromwell and Churchill)	74mm	68mm	60mm	47mm
57mm (towed)	–	81mm	64mm	50mm
76mm (towed, Sherman and Hellcat)	109mm	99mm	89mm	73mm
3in (Wolverine and towed)	109mm	99mm	89mm	73mm
British				
6pdr (towed)	143mm	131mm	117mm	90mm
17pdr (towed and Sherman Firefly)	149mm	140mm	130mm	111mm
German				
75mm KwK 40 (Panzer IV)	99mm	92mm	84mm	66mm
75mm PaK 40 (towed)	99mm	92mm	84mm	66mm
88mm KwK 36 (Panzer VIE Tiger)	120mm	112mm	102mm	88mm
75mm KwK 42 (Panzer V Panther)	138mm	128mm	118mm	100mm
88mm KwK 43 (Panzer VIB King Tiger, Jagdpanther and towed)	202mm	187mm	168mm	137mm
128mm PaK 44 (Jagdtiger)	–	212mm	202mm	182mm

FIELD, MEDIUM AND HEAVY ARTILLERY

	Weight of shell (lb)	Maximum range (yds)	Normal rate of fire per minute
USA			
75mm (airborne)	14	9,500	3
105mm SP or towed	33	12,150	3
155mm SP or towed	95	25,400	1 in 2 min
British			
25pdr SP or towed	25	13,400	3
4.5in towed	55	20,500	1
5.5in towed	80	18,100	1
7.2in	200	16,100	1 in 2 min
German			
105mm towed	32	10,675	3
150mm towed	95	12,300	1 in 2 min
210mm towed	264	33,900	1 in 3 min

British firepower. A 5.5in gun firing from its gun pit at the start of Operation "Greenline" on the night of 15 July. The pile of shells next to the gun is typical of an Allied opening barrage, even for a subsidiary operation. (IWM photograph B7413)

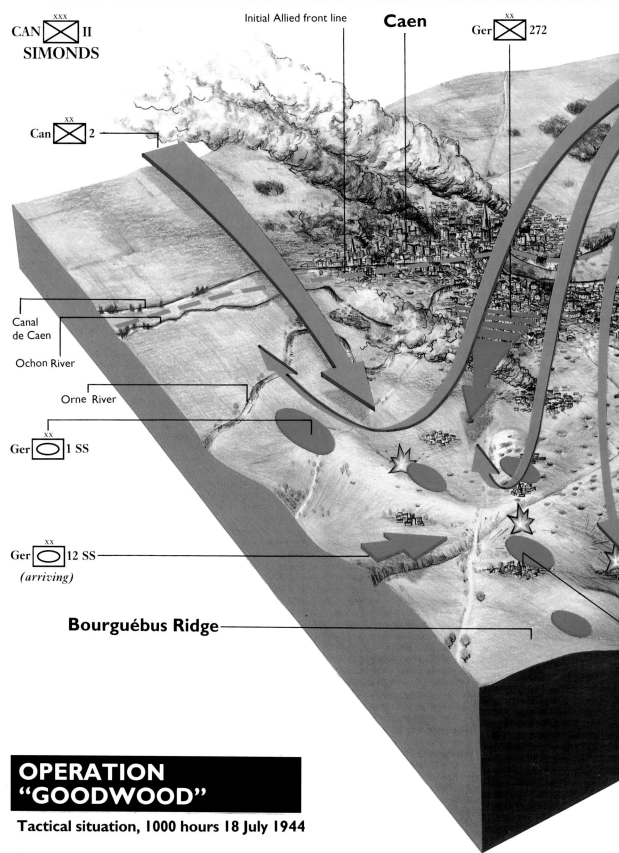

CAN ⊠ II
SIMONDS

Can ⊠ 2

Initial Allied front line

Caen

Ger ⊠ 272

Canal
de Caen

Ochon River

Orne River

Ger ⊡ 1 SS

Ger ⊡ 12 SS
(arriving)

Bourguébus Ridge

OPERATION "GOODWOOD"

Tactical situation, 1000 hours 18 July 1944

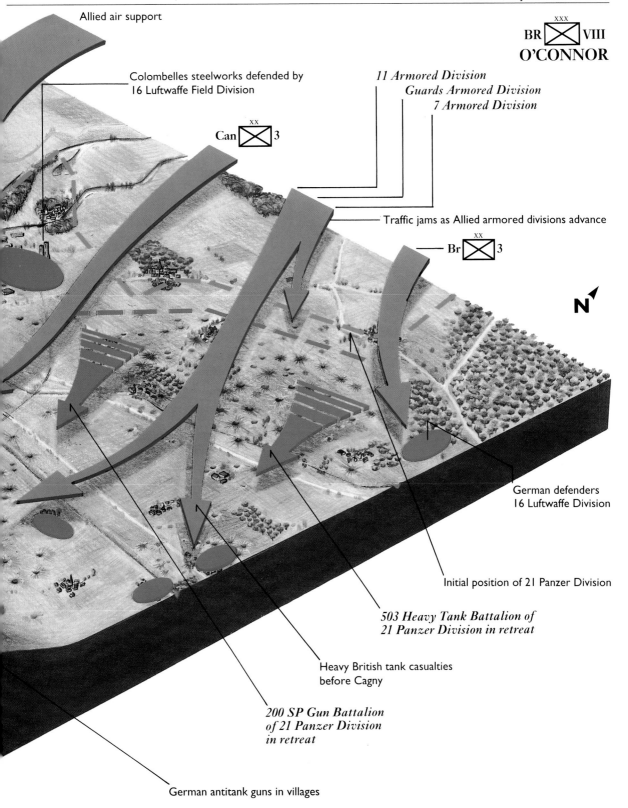

Allied air support

Colombelles steelworks defended by
16 Luftwaffe Field Division

Can ⊠ 3

BR ⊠ VIII
O'CONNOR

11 Armored Division
Guards Armored Division
7 Armored Division

Traffic jams as Allied armored divisions advance

Br ⊠ 3

N

German defenders
16 Luftwaffe Division

Initial position of 21 Panzer Division

503 Heavy Tank Battalion of
21 Panzer Division in retreat

Heavy British tank casualties
before Cagny

200 SP Gun Battalion
of 21 Panzer Division
in retreat

German antitank guns in villages

through the very constricted British front lines. The forward German zone was penetrated successfully, but Allied intelligence had underestimated the strength of the German defenses, which were almost ten miles (15km) deep: behind 16 Luftwaffe Field Division and 21 Panzer was a special self-propelled gun battalion, 200 Antitank Battalion, and 503 Heavy Tank Battalion of Tigers; behind them every village on the plain had its own group of four or five 88mm antitank guns, leading back to the main concentration of III Flak Corps on Bourgébus Ridge, with I SS Panzer Corps in reserve behind that. The structure of a British armored division, split between an infantry

Two M4 Shermans of 23 Hussars, the third tank regiment of 11 Armored Division, setting off at the start of Operation

"Goodwood," 18 July. Note the towers of the Colombelles steelworks in the distance. (IWM photograph B7524)

An aerial view of the area of the village of Cagny on 18 July at the start of Operation "Goodwood." The Allies bombed this area with heavy bombers, and although fuses were set to explode on impact the cratering was

considerable and greatly hampered the advance. The improvised defense of Cagny by five 88mm antitank guns and a few infantry was crucial to stopping the British advance. (IWM photograph CL477)

brigade and an armored brigade, meant that as the infantry were absorbed in clearing the first villages the tanks were advancing, virtually unsupported, into massed antitank guns. Just as Montgomery was announcing a complete success to SHAEF, and to the press, the armored drive was stopped in a mass of burning tanks short of Bourgébus Ridge. On the following day the infantry and tanks of both sides contested the villages on the forward slope of the ridge, and on 20 July the same torrential rain that had delayed Operation "Cobra" brought the offensive to a halt. Caen had been cleared and I SS Panzer Corps drawn back into the battle, but at the cost of 413 tanks, or 36 percent of Second British Army's tank strength. As Eisenhower put it, the British had advanced just seven miles (eleven km), at the rate of a thousand tons of bombs a mile.

It was then that Eisenhower showed the qualities that had made him Allied Supreme Commander. Despite pressure from Tedder, from his own staff and from every critic of Montgomery in the Allied war effort, he made no attempt to have Montgomery removed. Instead, he contented himself with a visit to Montgomery on 20 July, backed by a letter on the following day voicing his disappointment at the British failure and stressing that with the Germans too weak to launch a counterstroke the time for caution was over. Eisenhower could have taken over direct command himself. The date of 1 August had been set for the activation of Third U.S. Army and the formation of 12th Army Group; but, rather than change command in the middle of a battle, Eisenhower stipulated that Montgomery should remain in charge of both army groups until the battle was over. It was a difficult and entirely correct decision. Although Eisenhower had Churchill's full authority to remove any British commander he considered unsatisfactory, he knew how damaging it could be to the Allied coalition if he, as an American, sacked the most famous general in the British Army.

In fact, because of "Goodwood," Montgomery had now won his battle. On the evening of 18 July, Fifteenth Army's last armored division, 116 Panzer, was ordered to move to the Caen sector. The only two remaining German armored divisions in France, 9 Panzer and 11 Panzer, were away in the south. On the Caen front the British with three armored, ten infantry divisions and one airborne division faced seven armored and six infantry divisions. The Americans with four armored and thirteen infantry divisions faced two armored, one mechanized, three infantry, one air-landing and two parachute divisions. Even without the extreme weakness of the German forces, the American superiority was at least two to one.

Operation "Cobra," like "Goodwood," was based on the saturation bombing of the German line on a 7,000-yard front, very different from the previous American broad-front attacks, and an exploitation by armor. The target picked for 1,500 bombers of Eighth U.S. Air Force was "Panzer Lehr" Division, opposite Collins's VII Corps.

Operation "Goodwood," 18-20 July 1944

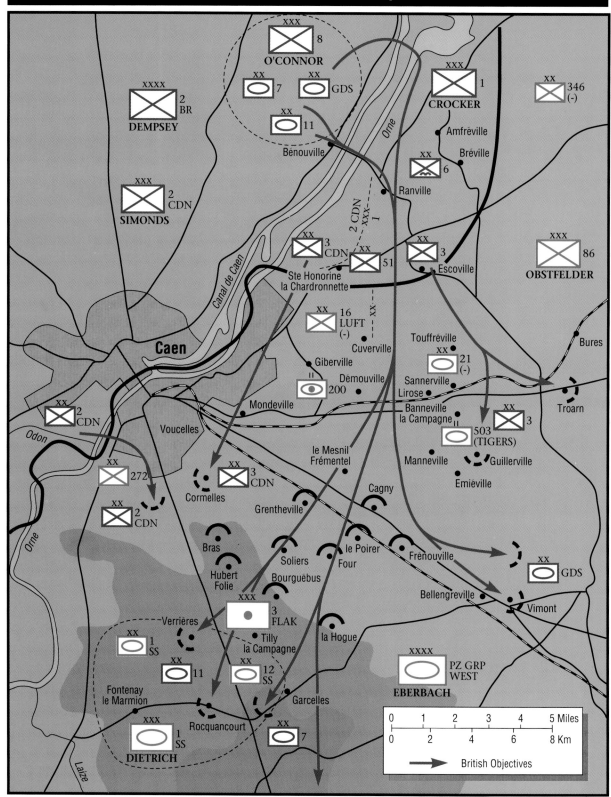

British Objectives

Goodwood result, 20 July 1944

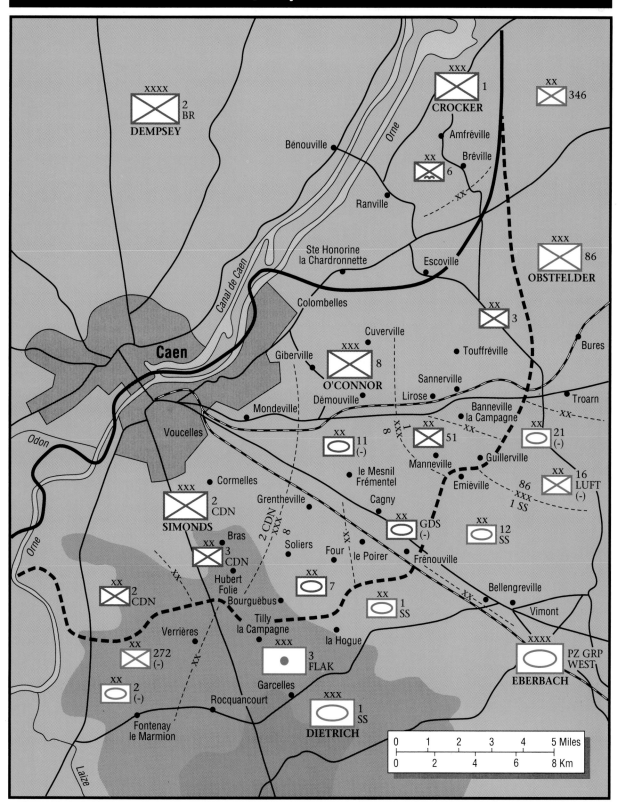

DEMPSEY 2 BR

CROCKER 1

346

Bénouville

Orne

6

Amfréville

Bréville

Ranville

Ste Honorine
la Chardronnette

Escoville

OBSTFELDER 86

Colombelles

Canal de Caen

Cuverville

3

Caen

Giberville

O'CONNOR 8

Touffréville

Bures

Sannerville

Lirose

Troarn

Démouville

Mondeville

Banneville
la Campagne

Voucelles

Odon

11 (-)

8

51

21 (-)

Manneville

Guillerville

Cormelles

le Mesnil
Frémentel

Emiéville

16
LUFT (-)

SIMONDS 2 CDN

Grentheville

Cagny

GDS (-)

12
SS

1 SS

86

1 SS

Bras

3 CDN

Soliers

Four

le Poirer

Frénouville

7

Bellengreville

2 CDN

Hubert
Folie

Bourguébus

Vimont

Tilly
la Campagne

la Hogue

272 (-)

Verrières

3 FLAK

EBERBACH PZ GRP WEST

2 (-)

Garcelles

Rocquancourt

1 SS

DIETRICH

Fontenay
le Marmion

Laize

0	1	2	3	4	5 Miles
0	2		4	6	8 Km

An M3 Stuart light tank of 2 (Armored) Battalion, Grenadier Guards, the leading battalion of the Guards Armored Division, at the start of Operation "Goodwood," 18 July. (It is confusing but typical of their approach that while two of the British armored divisions had tank formations made up from regiments of cavalry and the Royal Tank Regiment, the third had tank formations made up from battalions of converted foot guards.) The Stuart was a reconnaissance tank, too light for normal tank warfare. The British deployed twelve Stuarts with each of their tank regiments or battalions as a reconnaissance squadron. The Americans had one reconnaissance battalion of Stuarts and White armored cars with each armored division. (IWM photograph B7561)

A German Nebelwerfer, or multibarreled rocket launcher, of 7 Werfer Brigade shown loaded and ready to fire. This particular example is at Banneville-la-Campagne on the eastern flank of the "Goodwood" battle and was captured by 3 British Division on 20 July. As its name implies, the Nebelwerfer was originally intended for laying down smokescreens but proved highly effective as an area weapon. The distinctive sound of its firing led to its nickname of "Moaning Minnie" among the British. (IWM photograph B7783)

The secret of the successful British and Canadian use of air power was the system of Forward Air Controllers, RAF officers attached to each of the attacking divisions and able to talk directly through radio to the supporting aircraft as they came in to attack. Here Squadron Leader R. A. Sutherland, displaying both his nonregulation silk scarf and his Distinguished Flying Cross medal ribbon, confers with Major Colin Grey of the Queen's Regiment over a map board. The Major is wearing the formation flash of Second British Army and is on attached duties as a liaison officer. (IWM photograph CL565)

Unlike Dempsey, however, Bradley had infantry to spare. After the bombing, the attack would be made by three infantry divisions, holding the two armored divisions and one infantry division of the breakout force in reserve. Set for 24 July, "Cobra" was postponed at the last minute due to bad weather. The message did not get through to 335 aircraft, which bombed in poor visibility – in some places short, onto their own front-line troops. Remarkably, surprise was not lost, since the Germans considered that the American attack had been halted by their own retaliatory artillery fire.

Meanwhile, on 23 July, First Canadian Army was activated with II Canadian Corps and I British Corps under it. Lieutenant General Crerar planned his own offensive, Operation "Spring," to be launched on 25 July by II Canadian Corps down the Caen-Falaise road, with the Guards Armored Division and 7 Armored Division in reserve in case they broke through. So, by coincidence, on 25 July both offensives began

together. South of Caen the Canadians failed to make progress through the defenses of 1 SS Panzer and 9 SS Panzer, and after 24 hours the attack was called off. OB West, however, continued to regard "Spring" as the main Allied offensive for a further twelve hours before responding to "Cobra." In part this was because Collins's attack began so slowly, with American aircraft again bombing short onto their own troops. Among the dead was the highest-ranking Allied officer killed in Europe, Lieutenant General Lesley McNair, Chief of U.S. Ground Forces and in Normandy as, supposedly, Patton's replacement commanding FUSAG.

In the bombing, "Panzer Lehr" practically ceased to exist, losing all its tanks and two-thirds of its men. The infantry attack began at 1100, and by the end of the first day VII Corps had penetrated about 4,000 yards into the German position. On the following day VIII Corps to the west joined VII Corps in pushing the Germans back a further 8,000 yards, and on 27 July the break-

Operation "Cobra," 25 July 1944

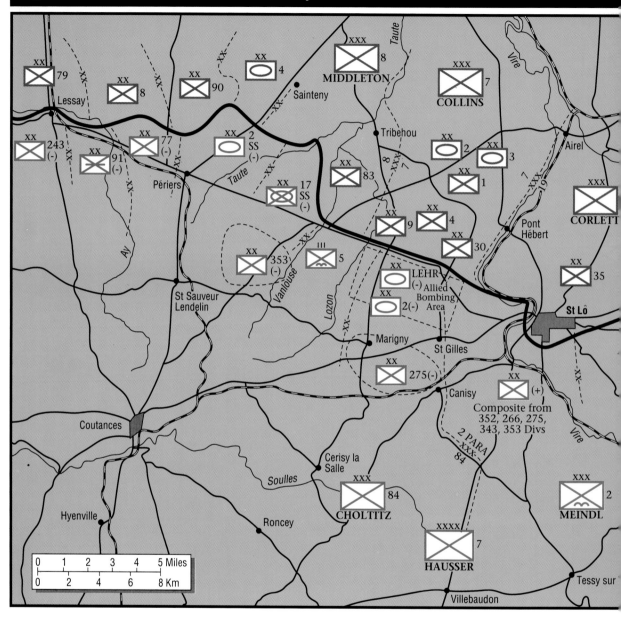

through came as 2 Armored Division (the "Hell on Wheels" division) fought its way through to open country. Bradley at once released VIII Corps into Patton's (theoretically nonexistent) command. On 28 July VII Corps captured Coutances, a penetration of more than twelve miles (seventeen km). Two days later, Patton's troops captured the crucial road junction at Avranches at the base of the Cotentin Peninsula, discovering that there was no coherent German opposition in front of them. On the following day, 1 August, Third U.S. Army became officially operational. Bradley took command of 12th Army Group with his deputy, Lieutenant General Courtney Hodges, taking over First U.S. Army. Within 24 hours, while air power and armor held open the five mile (eight km) gap at Avranches, Patton had passed four divisions through the town, out of the bocage, and onto the roads of France.

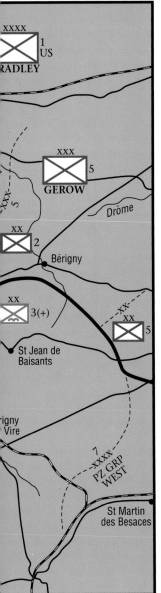

American infantry of VII Corps just south of St. Lô during or just before Operation "Cobra," late July. It was fighting in conditions such as these that slowed the American advance so much. The American troops are attempting to outflank an enemy position and have come under enemy artillery fire. (IWM photograph EA30511)

A soldier of 2 SS Panzer Division "Das Reich," probably from one of the division's two Panzergrenadier regiments, being searched by an infantryman of VIII Corps near the village of Gavray, south of Coutances, captured by the Americans on 30 July. (IWM photograph OWIL52255)

The Exploitation, 5 to 11 August

By the start of August, Oberstgruppenführer Hausser's Seventh Army was disintegrating. Panzer Group West, which was renamed Fifth Panzer Army on 5 August, followed it a week later. The numerical designations of German army corps and divisions remained, as did the neat boundaries on the maps, but on the ground there was only a collection of small battle groups, shrinking down to battalion size, made up of men who seldom knew where they were or who their divisional commander was that day. Where German units did stand and fight, their tactical superiority over the Allies was as pronounced as ever, preventing the retreat from becoming a rout until the very end. Even a small number of their superior tanks could bring an Allied pursuit to a sudden halt. But after 11 August nobody on either side in Normandy imagined that the Germans could win the battle.

As the German front broke and the battle became mobile, German commanders were forced to rely more on radio transmissions, releasing more information to the Allies through "Ultra." The Allied tactical air forces also came fully into play as the weather improved, attacking German columns on the move and causing horrible losses in the horsed transport on which they relied. Most German units were short of ammunition, particularly for their antitank guns; and tanks, and other vehicles were being abandoned on the battlefield for lack of fuel. By 6 August, Army Group B had taken 144,261 casualties and received only 19,914 replacements.

On 27 July, finally realizing that "Cobra" and not "Spring" was the main Allied threat, von Kluge attempted to seal the gap. By the next day LVIII Panzer Corps headquarters was on its way

Lieutenant General George S. Patton displaying his equally famous bad teeth and ivory-handled revolvers to General Montgomery shortly after his arrival in France in early July. Lieutenant General Bradley is between Patton and Montgomery – as he often found himself in their disputes. Patton was regarded by the Germans as the best of the Allied commanders and shared many of their characteristics in his approach to battle, but he was bad at coping with the complex politics of the war. Note that none of the generals wear formation signs or distinguishing insignia other than their rank badges. (IWM photograph B6551)

from the south, so freeing XLVII Panzer Corps headquarters, which pulled out of line opposite the British and began to take 2 Panzer and 116 Panzer westward, slowly for want of fuel, to confront VII U.S. Corps at Avranches. By 1 August, 9 Panzer Division and six infantry divisions, in various states of readiness, were also heading for the Normandy battlefield. Although there was no exact moment when the Germans saw through "Fortitude," these moves marked the end of any remaining value in the deception plan. Unable to get a coherent report from the front, von Kluge replaced the commander of LXXXIV Corps, sacked Seventh Army's chief of staff, and on 30 July briefly took over command of Seventh Army himself.

The object of "Cobra," as laid down in the original "Overlord" plan, had been to secure the ports of Brittany. The German decision not to retreat from the bocage, and Montgomery's skill in preventing them from forming a reserve, meant that when the break came it was far more complete than the Allies had originally expected. For the rest of the battle, their own success seemed to catch them off balance. On 29 July, Bradley ordered Patton to turn the whole of Middleton's VIII Corps westward into Brittany while the remainder of Third U.S. Army drove for Mortain. Middleton's two armored and two infantry divisions were opposed by XXV Corps with troops from six divisions, including the re-formed 77 Division and 91 Airlanding Division. In fact, "Cobra" actually failed in its original intention of securing the Brittany ports, some of which did not fall until September, and like Cherbourg they were of no immediate value to the Allies. Bradley was criticized for failing to turn VIII Corps, his leading formation, eastward toward Paris at once, but to have done so might have invited the counterstroke against Third U.S. Army's flank or rear that Eisenhower, Montgomery and Bradley all feared. Patton, typically, would later say that if he had worried about his flanks he could never have fought the war.

To accompany "Cobra," Bradley had ordered V U.S. Corps, on the boundary with Second British Army, to launch a diversionary attack on 26 July; this was making slow progress. Mont-gomery, meanwhile, had sidestepped Guards Armored Division and 7 Armored Division westward after the failure of Operation "Spring." On 30 July, with air and artillery support, O'Connor's VIII Corps of two armored divisions and one infantry division attacked toward Vire alongside V U.S. Corps, while Bucknall's XXX Corps drove for Mont Pinçon, in Operation "Bluecoat." This front, the worst of the Suisse Normande country, was held by LXXIV Corps headquarters, which had also arrived from Brittany. On 2 August (with echoes of Operation "Epsom") von Kluge pulled II SS Panzer Corps out of line in the east and committed it against O'Connor's advance, which was stopped two miles (three km) short of Vire. Progress by XXX Corps was so slow that Mont-gomery replaced Bucknall with Lieutenant General Brian Horrocks, who had commanded XXX Corps for him in the Western Desert. Mont Pinçon was finally secured on 6 August, the same day that XIX U.S. Corps, attacking alongside the British, captured Vire.

Patton's Third U.S. Army, meanwhile, had been advancing almost unopposed. By 1 August the lead elements of VIII Corps had reached Rennes. On 3 August, Bradley, with Mont-gomery's approval, ordered Patton to divert only minimum forces into Brittany and to send the rest of Third U.S. Army eastward. By 8 August, Patton's newly formed XV Corps was at Le Mans, outflanking LVIII Panzer Corps and LXXXI Corps (little more than 9 Panzer Division and some battle groups). At the same time, XX Corps was racing due south for Nantes, with XII Corps forming behind it. This was the time for American mobility to prove itself.

On 3 August, Adolf Hitler, rejecting numerous requests from von Kluge for a retreat, ordered that the line between the Orne and Vire Rivers should be taken over entirely by infantry divisions, freeing at least four armored divisions for a counterattack westward across the base of the Cotentin Peninsula to Avranches, cutting Patton's forces in half and bottling up the Allied breakout. With II SS Panzer Corps committed against the British at Vire, XLVII Panzer Corps headquarters was appointed to coordinate the attack, which was made by the remnants of 2 Panzer Division,

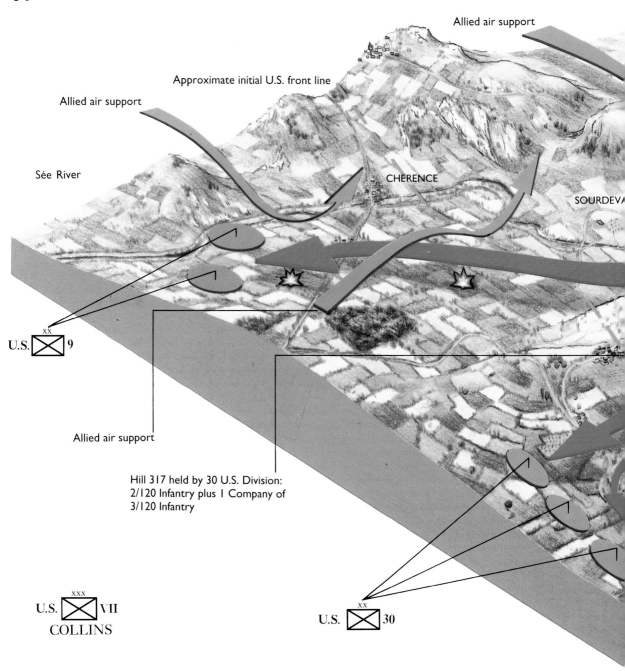

N

Allied air support

Approximate initial U.S. front line

Allied air support

Sée River

CHERENCE

SOURDEVA

U.S. ⊠ 9

Allied air support

Hill 317 held by 30 U.S. Division:
2/120 Infantry plus I Company of
3/120 Infantry

U.S. ⊠ VII
COLLINS

U.S. ⊠ 30

MORTAIN COUNTERATTACK

Dawn, 0500 hours 7 August 1944

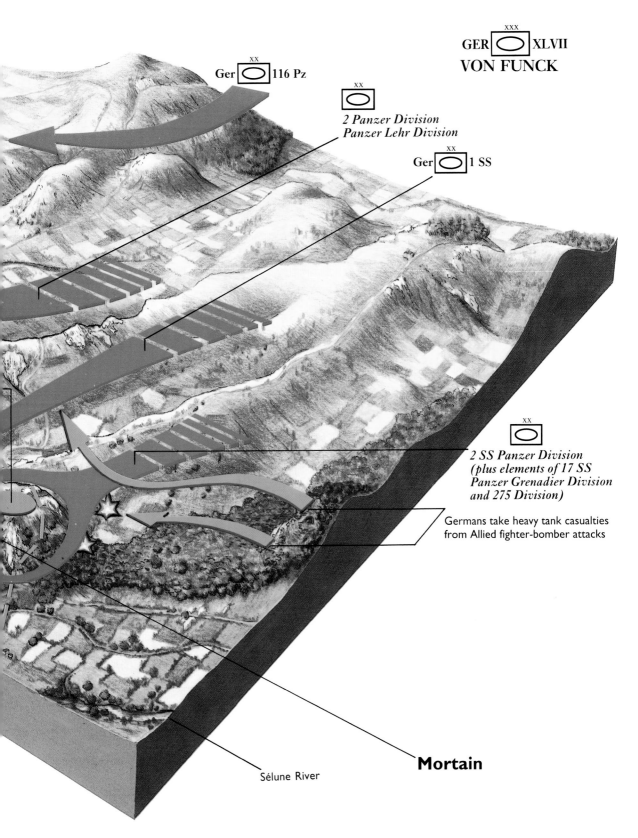

GER ⬭ XLVII
VON FUNCK

Ger ⬭ 116 Pz

⬭
2 Panzer Division
Panzer Lehr Division

Ger ⬭ 1 SS

⬭
2 SS Panzer Division
(plus elements of 17 SS
Panzer Grenadier Division
and 275 Division)

Germans take heavy tank casualties
from Allied fighter-bomber attacks

Mortain

Sélune River

"Panzer Lehr" Division, 1 SS Panzer Division, 2 SS Panzer Division, 116 Panzer Division and 17 SS Panzergrenadier Division – in all, no more than 185 tanks. The attack, codenamed "Lüttich" (German for the town of Liège in Belgium), would start at Mortain, held by First U.S. Army's VII Corps. This was just the sort of mobile armored attack that Rommel had declared impossible against Allied air power, and nobody except Hitler had any faith in its success. The commander of 116 Panzer was sacked for refusing to let his division take part.

"Ultra" gave the Allies a few hours' warning of the Mortain counterattack, which began on the

night of 6 August, striking 30 U.S. Division. By this date, nearly the whole Allied tactical air strength was in Normandy, and Eisenhower assured Bradley that, even if the Germans broke through, his troops could be both supplied and supported by air. Although the Germans captured Mortain itself, they failed to secure the crucial high ground east of the town, Hill 317, which was held by a reinforced battalion of 30 Division, and at dawn they came under repeated British and American fighter-bomber attack. Perhaps 70 German tanks penetrated VII Corps front, of which 30 remained by that evening. The five armored divisions had left between them eight 88mm anti-tank guns, and had run out of fuel after advancing no more than five miles (eight km). On 9 August, Hitler, despite further protests from both von Kluge and Hausser, ordered XLVII Panzer Corps to hold in place. General Eberbach was to relinquish command of Fifth Panzer Army to Obergruppenführer Dietrich of I SS Panzer Corps, and

The start of Operation "Bluecoat." Men and Bren carriers of 4 Battalion, Wiltshire Regiment, 43 (Wessex) Division, on 31 July in the dust, heat and congestion typical of the

Suisse Normande. The sergeant in the foreground appears to be a regimental traffic policeman, who would be responsible for the smooth flow of traffic behind the lines. (IWM photograph B8308)

to concentrate all of Army Group B's available armor into a new command, Panzer Group Eberbach. Of Army size, this would come administratively under Hausser's Seventh Army and would attack on 11 August, first southwestward, and then northwestward all the way back to Avranches.

The Encirclement, 11 to 25 August

Through "Ultra," the Allies knew within 24 hours that the Germans would not retreat from Mortain. On 6 August, Montgomery had issued a directive for a long envelopment against an organized Ger-

man retreat. First Canadian Army would open an offensive southward toward Falaise and then turn eastward toward the Seine River. Second British Army would drive southeast for Argentan and then also turn eastward. Bradley's 12th Army Group was to continue its advance eastward and then northeast toward Paris. The failure of "Lüttich" opened up the possibility of a "short hook" to envelop the whole of Army Group B where it stood. On 8 August, Bradley, having conferred with Montgomery and Eisenhower, ordered Patton to turn his XV Corps northward to Alençon as the southern arm of the encirclement, while VII Corps drove the remnant of XLVII Panzer Corps back. On 11 August Montgomery issued a new directive: the Canadians were to capture Falaise and Argentan while 12th Army Group moved up from Alençon to Argentan to complete the circle. Montgomery, ever cautious, expressed concern about the strength of the German armor still in the Mortain area.

The linkup between 3 British Division and 2 U.S. Division just north of Vire on 3 August, providing a firm shoulder for the exploitation by Third U.S. Army. Here a soldier of 2 U.S. Division walks over to talk to the gun crew of a British 6pdr antitank gun. Note the formation flashes for both divisions, and the Bren gun on the right. The ground in the distance is typical of the Suisse Normande. (IWM photograph B8985)

The Breakout, 16 August 1944

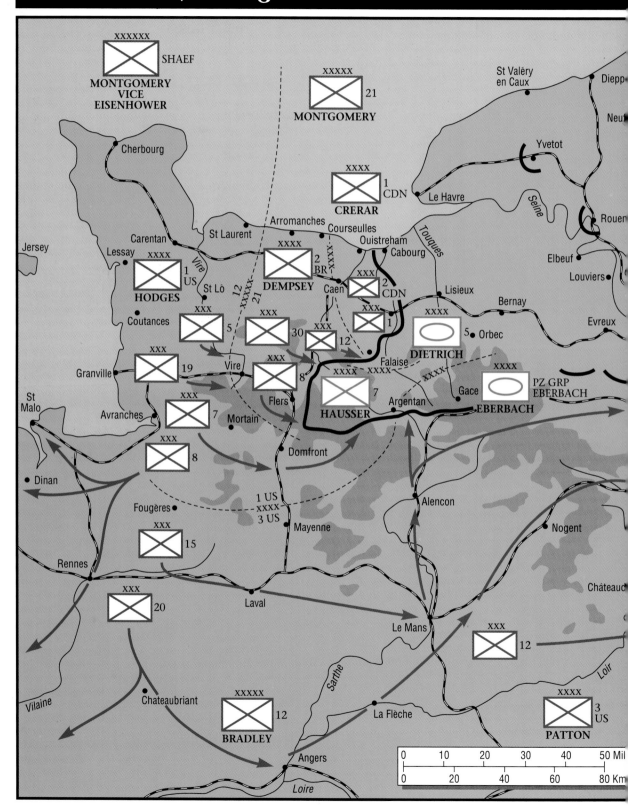

Sergeant Major McCulloch of 6 Battalion, Royal Scots Fusiliers, 15 (Scottish) Division, advancing through a cornfield during "Bluecoat," 3 August. By this date 15 Division was a veteran formation that had been in action for more than six weeks, and it is instructive to note that the sergeant major is carrying a rifle, with bayonet fixed, rather than a submachine gun. He has also either removed or dirtied down the formation flashes on his shoulders, and is indistinguishable from a private. (IWM photograph B8558)

The Canadian attack south from Caen, Operation "Totalize," began on the night of 7 August. With support from RAF Bomber Command, II Canadian Corps attacked against 89 Division, hastily reinforced by 12 SS Panzer. Lieutenant General Crerar's reserves, 4 Canadian Armored Division and 1 Polish Armored Division, were new to battle and to Normandy, and made slow progress. One Canadian armored regiment lost its way altogether and was overrun by the Germans. Despite their considerably superior numbers, the Canadians were halted on 11 August after an advance of nine miles (fifteen km), only halfway to Falaise.

On the following day the leading elements of XV U.S. Corps (two infantry and two armored divisions, including 2 French Armored Division) reached Argentan. On 14 August, First Canadian Army launched its renewed offensive, Operation

79

"Tractable," and three days later broke through to Falaise, twelve miles (eighteen km) north of the American positions. Seventh Army, Panzer Group Eberbach and most of Fifth Panzer Army were being squeezed into a giant pocket, from which the Falaise gap was the only exit.

Despite the slow Canadian progress, Bradley turned down Patton's request on 13 August to push XV Corps north of Argentan and close the pocket, so provoking another controversy. Third U.S. Army's swing northward had squeezed out most of First U.S. Army, and XV Corps was ordered to hold in place until its line at Argentan could be taken over by First U.S. Army troops. Bradley once more preferred not to risk a counter-stroke against both sides of his thinly stretched line if he drove north to Falaise. The Germans had plenty of experience in being surrounded, by Soviet forces on the Eastern Front, but never before accompanied by the kind of air-power that

A Sherman Firefly of 1 Polish Armored Division waiting to go into action during Operation "Totalize," 8 August. The "PL" formation sign was used along with the "Winged Hussar" of Poland. The division was equipped and organized by the British and made up of

Poles who had escaped to Britain in 1939. By a grim coincidence, 1 Polish Armored was committed to battle in Normandy a few days after the start of the ultimately unsuccessful Warsaw uprising against the Germans. (IWM photograph B8826)

the Allies could bring against their steadily shrinking battle groups. The Allies, on the other hand, had no training or experience in conducting such an encirclement. While their forces were being wiped out from the air, German tactical superiority, and Allied respect for it, prevented the pocket being closed on the ground.

Whatever was happening in Normandy, Adolf Hitler continued to direct the battle from Rasten-

Even after the Germans had been driven from their prepared defenses they used the farmhouses and small villages of Normandy as strongpoints. These are British troops of VIII Corps training in farmhouse fighting and sniper clearance on 10 August, experiencing the same problems that were holding up the Canadians in their drive toward Falaise. Note that by this stage in the battle infantry have largely dispensed with regimental and divisional flashes, and that far more automatic weapons are being carried: in this case two Sten submachine guns between three men. (IWM photograph B8964)

M3 Stuart light tanks, the leading elements of a division of XV U.S. Corps, enter the village of Luce sur Ballon near Falaise on 14 or 15 August. The village, with its church steeple and apple orchards, is typical of this region of Normandy. (IWM photograph EA34030)

The Falaise Pocket, 16 August 1944

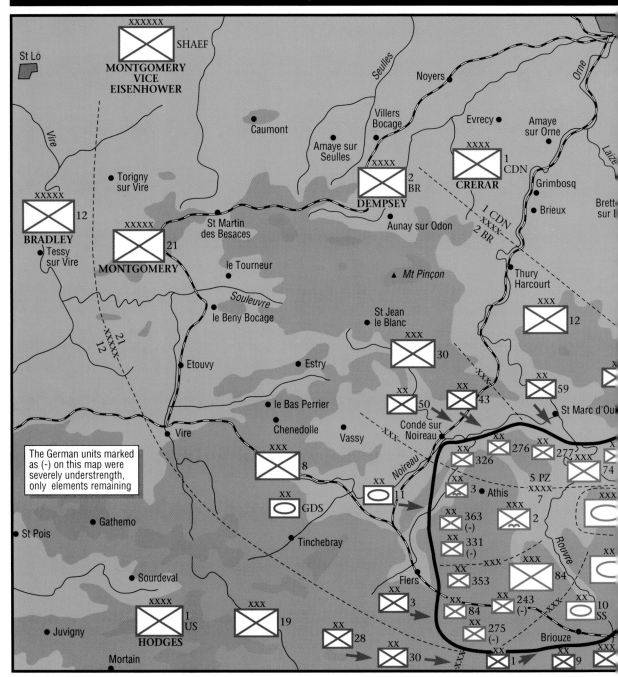

The German units marked as (-) on this map were severely understrength, only elements remaining

burg as if victory were still possible. By 12 August, Panzer Group Eberbach had assembled on the southern shoulder of the pocket at Argentan. But, as the German front collapsed, what had been intended as a decisive armored counterstroke against XV U.S. Corps resolved itself into no more than a reinforcement of 45 tanks and 4,000 men. On 15 August, Generalfeldmarschall von Kluge, driving between headquarters, was attacked by an Allied fighter-bomber and went missing in the pocket. Hitler placed Hausser in temporary command of Army Group B.

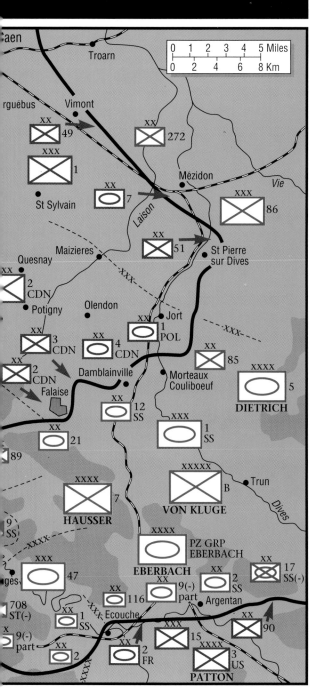

Group G to strengthen the Normandy front meant that it was the "Dragoon" forces that had the easier path. On his reappearance at his own headquarters, von Kluge informed OKW that the Falaise pocket could not be held, and on 16 August Hitler finally agreed to a withdrawal. The decision had come far too late, although any attempt to withdraw earlier would also have produced heavy German casualties. On 17 August renewed drives by II Canadian Corps and V U.S. Corps brought the jaws of the pocket to within a few thousand yards of each other, and by 20 August, despite repeated German attacks from both sides, the pocket was closed. On 18 August Hitler replaced von Kluge as Commander OB West and Army Group B with Generalfeld-marschall Walther Model, who found himself in charge of a rout. Summoned to Rastenburg, von Kluge committed suicide. Oberstgruppenführer Hausser was badly wounded on 20 August, losing

For some of Patton's men the drive across France was hardly a race. These are infantry of XX U.S. Corps just west of Chartres on 17 August. Veterans have removed all identifying insignia from their uniforms, and new arrivals as casualty replacements have not bothered to add them. Leading is the platoon lieutenant, followed by his sergeant (note the binocular case), the radio man and the BAR man. The damage done to the area by the fighting is obvious from this picture. (IWM photograph EA34627)

On the same day, which Hitler later called the worst of his life, Operation "Dragoon," the Allied landing in the south of France, took place. Intended as a supporting action for "Overlord," it was now too late to have any relevance to the Battle of Normandy. Indeed, the stripping of Army

an eye. He escaped from the pocket, but Seventh Army as a command ceased to exist. Eberbach shepherded the remaining German formations eastward before himself being captured on 30 August.

By 22 August all resistance in the Falaise pocket had ceased. Eisenhower, two days later, recorded that it was possible to walk for hundreds of yards on nothing but dead and decaying flesh. The smell penetrated the cockpits of aircraft flying overhead. The Allies had great difficulty in assessing how much destruction they had caused. Perhaps 10,000 enemy troops had been killed, 50,000 surrendered, and 20,000 had escaped. By no means all of these were German; in the last stages of the attack 1 Polish

Armored had carried with it truckloads of British uniforms into which Polish-born prisoners from the Ost battalions could change before resuming the fight against their old masters. The Allies counted 567 tanks or self-propelled guns, over 950 artillery pieces and 7,700 other vehicles wrecked and abandoned in the pocket. Of 38 German divisions committed to the battle, 25 had been completely destroyed. Between them, the eight battle groups of 2 Panzer, 21 Panzer, 116 Panzer, 1 SS Panzer, 2 SS Panzer, 9 SS Panzer, 10 SS Panzer and 12 SS Panzer now mustered 70 tanks, 36 artillery pieces and fourteen weak infantry battalions. "Panzer Lehr" and 9 Panzer had been wiped out. The same, for all practical purposes, was true

of Army Group B. Divisions that were not crushed had been broken up and dispersed. Advancing eastward, XII British Corps found that it was taking prisoners from thirteen different divisions on its front.

Of over a million men who had fought under Rommel, von Kluge and Model in Normandy, 240,000 were dead or wounded, a further 200,000 missing or captured. The Germans had lost 1,500 tanks, 3,500 artillery pieces, 20,000 vehicles and over 3,600 aircraft. Nobody could count the number of dead horses, or wanted to do so. By the end of August the Allies had landed in Normandy 39 divisions or 2,052,299 men, along with 438,471 vehicles and 3,098,259 tons of stores. They had

suffered 209,672 casualties including 36,976 dead. Altogether 4,101 Allied aircraft and 16,714 aircrew had been lost over the battlefield or in support of the battle.

On 17 August, XV U.S. Corps had handed over the front at Argentan to V U.S. Corps and joined the rest of Third U.S. Army racing eastward. On the night of 19 August, Patton's leading division, 79 Division, crossed the Seine River. By 25 August all four Allied armies were level with the Seine, and on that day 2 French Armored Division liberated Paris. The date was D-Day plus 80 days, or just slightly ahead of schedule for Montgomery's original "Overlord" plan. The Battle of Normandy was over.

Even the Germans who escaped the Falaise pocket were not safe from Allied air power. Here German columns have been caught on the road near the village of Clinchamps, about seven miles (twelve km) east of Falaise, by aircraft of Second Tactical Air Force on 19 August. Smoke is rising from vehicles hit on the road while others are trying to escape across country. Note the bomb craters already marking the ground from a previous raid. (IWM photograph CL838)

Allied soldiers attempting to assess the wreckage of German vehicles in or close to the Falaise pocket, probably in early September. Canadian and American troops are clearing the debris out of the way, and any bodies have been removed for burial. In the foreground is probably the burned-out remains of a German half-track. Ground conditions in the pocket varied from open country to the bocage shown in this picture. (IWM photograph CL909)

Dead horses of German transport in the Falaise pocket, 25 August. In Normandy the complete motorization of the Allied forces gave them a marked advantage over the Germans, who rarely showed horses in their own official films or photographs but were nevertheless heavily dependent on them for their transport throughout the war. (IWM photograph B9668)

White armored cars of 2 French Armored Division on parade in the Champs Elysees on the afternoon of 25 August as crowds celebrate the liberation of Paris. The concerned looks of the crews may be due to the fact that sniping and streetfighting were still going on not far from them at the time. (IWM photograph BU124)

THE AFTERMATH OF THE BATTLE

On 1 September 1944 Eisenhower took over formal command of all SHAEF ground forces in Europe from Montgomery, to the latter's intense frustration. In compensation, Churchill promoted Montgomery to Field Marshal, one rank higher than Eisenhower, for whom the new five-star rank of General of the Army was then quickly invented. Meanwhile the Allied spearheads were advancing virtually unopposed toward Germany. Third U.S. Army liberated Chalons-sur-Marne on 29 August, and on 31 August its leading tanks crossed the Meuse River at Verdun. On 3 September, Second British Army liberated Brussels, with Antwerp following a day later. Commanders talked with some optimism of ending the war in one or two months.

Eisenhower was faced at once with a difficult decision. German garrisons still held the ports of Brittany and the Pas de Calais, and all Allied supplies were still coming across the Normandy beaches. Logistics planners advised that the available supplies could not support all four armies at such a rate of advance. The original "Overlord" strategy of a broad front had been based on the fear that the Germans might counterattack a narrow thrust. Montgomery now pressed Eisenhower, to the verge of insubordination and beyond, to abandon this strategy, halt Third U.S. Army, and give priority to a northern drive to be made by Second British Army with First U.S. Army in support. Within a week, Patton, with Bradley's support, was pressing for the opposite strategy, to give priority to his own Third U.S. Army driving into eastern France. Both hoped to get across the Rhine and into the German industrial heartland of the Ruhr before Christmas.

It was not apparent to Eisenhower, however, that Allied supplies could support even one army on such a drive. For reasons of coalition solidarity and safety he took the politically correct but strategically controversial decision to continue the broad front strategy. The normally cautious Montgomery, trying to force Eisenhower's hand, attempted to seize a bridgehead over the Rhine in Operation "Market Garden" on 17 September, in which three divisions of First Allied Airborne Army dropped to form a "carpet" through northern Holland along which XXX British Corps could advance to Arnhem. The operation was a disastrous failure, Montgomery's first and only defeat in a major battle. Characteristically, he described it as a 90 percent success. By the end of September lack of fuel had slowed the whole Allied advance, giving the Germans time to strengthen their lines, and it was not until a renewed campaign in the spring that the Rhine was finally crossed. But after the Battle of Normandy the only question was how soon the war would end, not who would win it. Germany surrendered unconditionally to the Allies on 8 May 1945.

Too much discussion on Normandy has centered on the controversial decisions of the Allied commanders. It was not good enough, apparently, to win such a complete and spectacular victory over an enemy that had conquered most of Europe unless it was done perfectly. Most of the blame for this lies with Montgomery, who was foolish enough to insist that it *had* been done perfectly, that Normandy – and all his other battles – had been fought according to a precise master plan drawn up beforehand, from which he never deviated. It says much for his personality that Montgomery found others to agree with him, despite overwhelming evidence to the contrary. His handling of the Battle of Normandy was of a very high order, and as the person who would certainly have been blamed for losing the battle, he deserves the credit for winning it. Credit should also go to Eisenhower for his skill as a political leader. (In

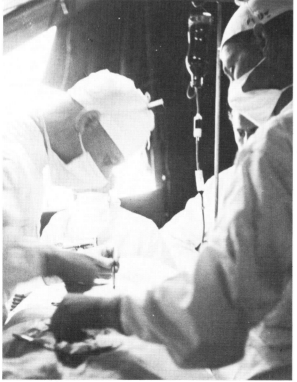

The reason for the battle. French refugees returning to their homes in Normandy. This particular photograph was taken on 5 July. Their transport is a civilian truck commandeered by the Germans and painted with military camouflage, now reacquired by the locals and being pulled by two horses. Note the small boy's British steel helmet. (IWM photograph B6483)

The price of the battle. Major C. J. Gordon of the Royal Army Medical Corps performs an operation at Number 32 Casualty Clearing Station, I British Corps, area near Reviers, on 20 June. (IWM photograph B5907)

The price of the battle. A very young, dead machine gunner of 25 SS Panzergrenadier Regiment, 12 SS Panzer Division, beside a trench in Malon, Normandy, 9 July. (IWM photograph B6807)

1952 he was to be elected President of the United States and to serve two terms of office.) Those German commanders who survived the war were happy to blame their defeat on Adolf Hitler. Some, with incredible arrogance, even tried to lecture the men who had so thoroughly defeated them on how they themselves might have done it better.

Could the Germans have won the Battle of Normandy? They might have had better intelligence developed, to see through Operation "Fortitude." They might have rationalized their command structure and improved their supplies and training. The Allies would not have invaded without air superiority, but it has been suggested that the Germans could have won at least air parity after D-Day by producing and employing as fighters a significant number of their Me 262 jet aircraft, which were already in service. The Germans might have mixed armor in with their weaker infantry formations, raising the overall standard at the expense of a few "showcase" divisions. They might have built the submarines or surface vessels to cut the vital sea link across the English Channel. There is much that they might have done. But in the actual circumstances of the battle as it

developed, there was nothing they could have done to win it. At the level that the Battle of Normandy was fought, the art of generalship consisted of not letting such circumstances arise. The dispute between Rommel and von Rundstedt over a rigid or a flexible defensive strategy was a massive irrelevance. Nor did any of their replacements have anything better to suggest. In truth, German generalship in Normandy was of a low order throughout the battle. Patton, who was killed in a road accident in 1945, could have given them all lessons in inventiveness, and in how to get results by disobeying orders.

Below the highest command level, Allied air power and artillery were the key factors in winning the Battle of Normandy, but they did not win it alone. Cutting off supplies and reinforcements to the German front line was only of value if, at the same time, the Allies were attacking and forcing the Germans to use up their reserves. Inferior in quality to the best German troops, likely to identify every tank they saw as a Tiger, the Allied infantry and tank crews showed great courage in maintaining the offensive. A large part of the German strength, however, came from the country in which they were fighting. Like the trenches of the First World War or the jungles of the Pacific, the bocage itself became a formidable enemy. It is noteworthy that the Germans themselves had rather less success attacking through it than the Allies, and once without its protection they collapsed at great speed.

It is a commonplace that an army reflects its society. Having seldom lost a war, the British Army, in false modesty, likes to praise its opponents and denigrate itself. They were almost the best troops in the world, it seems to suggest, what a pity they were facing us. The American style is more of self-praise at the expense of all others, conceding merit to an opponent before a rival. The German approach turns war into a morality play, the tragic defeat of mere mortals struggling with superhuman strength against the impersonal forces of the machine. If the Americans had been as good as they said they were, the British as bad as they said they were, and the Germans as good as everyone said they were, the Battle of Normandy could not have been fought as it was.

CHRONOLOGY

3 September 1939 Britain and France declare war on Germany.

10 May 1940 Germany attacks France and the Low Countries.

3 June 1940 Last British troops evacuated from France.

10 June 1940 Italy declares war on Britain and France.

22 June 1940 France signs an armistice with Germany.

22 June 1941 Germany and the Axis powers declare war on the Soviet Union.

7 December 1941 Pearl Harbor. Japan declares war on Britain and the United States.

12 December 1941 Germany declares war on the United States.

19 August 1942 The Dieppe Raid, the first Allied amphibious landing of the war, results in disaster.

8 November 1942 Operation "Torch," the Anglo-American amphibious landings in North Africa.

10 November 1942 Germany occupies Vichy France.

10 July 1943 Operation "Husky," the Allied amphibious landing in Sicily.

8 September 1943 Operation "Avalanche," the Allied amphibious landing in Italy. Unconditional surrender of Italy.

6 December 1943 Eisenhower appointed as Supreme Commander, Allied Expeditionary Force, for Operation "Overlord," the invasion of France.

22 January 1944 Operation "Shingle," the Allied amphibious landing at Anzio.

15 May 1944 Final SHAEF planning conference for Operation "Overlord."

6 June 1944 D-DAY FOR OPERATION "OVERLORD," THE START OF THE BATTLE OF NORMANDY.

11 June 1944 Hitler directive forbidding any German retreat.

12 June 1944 First U.S. Army captures Carentan.

13 June 1944 Second British Army held at Villers Bocage. First V-1 flying bombs hit London and southern England.

16 June 1944 Hitler directive to reinforce Normandy.

17 June 1944 First U.S. Army captures Barneville on the west coast of the Cotentin Peninsula. Hitler visits Rommel and von Rundstedt at Soissons.

19–22 June 1944 "The Great Storm."

25 June 1944 Operation "Dauntless" by XXX British Corps.

26–30 June 1944 Operation "Epsom" by VIII British Corps.

27 June 1944 The port of Cherbourg surrenders to VII U.S. Corps.

28 June 1944 Generaloberst Friedrich Dollmann, commanding Seventh Army, commits suicide and is replaced by Oberstgruppenführer Paul Hausser.

2 July 1944 Generalfeldmarschall Gerd von Rundstedt replaced at OB West by Generalfeldmarschall Günther von Kluge.

3 July 1944 First U.S. Army starts an offensive southward toward St. Lô.

6 July 1944 General Leo Freiherr Geyr von Schweppenburg replaced at Panzer Group West by General Heinrich Eberbach.

7–8 July 1944 Operation "Charnwood" by I British Corps captures northern Caen.

10 July 1944 Operation "Jupiter" by VIII British Corps. Montgomery directive on the breakout into Brittany.

15 July 1944 Operation "Greenline" by XXX British Corps and XII British Corps.

17 July 1944 Generalfeldmarschall Erwin Rommel wounded and replaced at Army Group B by Generalfeldmarschall Günther von Kluge, who also continues as Commander OB West.

18–20 July 1944 Operation "Goodwood" by VIII British Corps, II Canadian Corps and I British Corps captures the remainder of Caen.

19 July 1944 First U.S. Army captures St. Lô.

20 July 1944 The "Bomb Plot" attempt to assassinate Hitler.

23 July 1944 First Canadian Army becomes operational.

24 July 1944 "False start" for Operation "Cobra" by VII U.S. Corps.

25–28 July 1944 Operation "Cobra" by VII U.S. Corps breaks out of the bocage.

25 July 1944 Operation "Spring" by II Canadian Corps.

30 July 1944 Operation "Bluecoat" by Second British Army. First U.S. Army captures Avranches.

1 August 1944 12th Army Group and Third U.S. Army become operational

3 August 1944 Hitler directive for defending Normandy by counterstroke.

5 August 1944 Panzer Group West renamed Fifth Panzer Army.

6 August 1944 Montgomery directive for a deep encirclement of Army Group B.

6–8 August 1944 Operation "Lüttich" by XLVII Panzer Corps, the Mortain counterattack.

8–11 August 1944 Operation "Totalize" by First Canadian Army. Bradley turns XV U.S. Corps north for the "short hook" encirclement.

9 August 1944 Hitler directive ordering the creation of Panzer Group Eberbach, while XLVII Panzer Corps holds its position. Oberstgruppenführer "Sepp" Dietrich takes temporary command of Fifth Panzer Army.

12 August 1944 XV U.S. Corps captures Argentan.

14–17 August 1944 Operation "Tractable" by First Canadian Army.

15 August 1944 Operation "Dragoon," the Allied amphibious landing in the south of France.

16 August 1944 Hitler agrees to a withdrawal of Seventh Army.

17 August 1944 First Canadian Army captures Falaise.

18 August 1944 Generalfeldmarschall Günther von Kluge replaced at OB West and Army Group B by Generalfeldmarschall Walther Model, and commits suicide.

19 August 1944 Third U.S. Army starts to cross the Seine River.

20 August 1944 Falaise pocket closed by First Canadian Army and First U.S. Army. Oberstgruppenführer Paul Hausser injured. General Heinrich Eberbach takes temporary command of Seventh Army.

22 August 1944 Falaise pocket wiped out.

25 August 1944 2 French Armored Division liberates Paris. **END OF THE BATTLE OF NORMANDY.**

29 August 1944 Third U.S. Army crosses the Marne River.

30 August 1944 Third U.S. Army crosses the Meuse River.

1 September 1944 General Eisenhower takes command of SHAEF ground forces from Montgomery, who is promoted to Field Marshal.

3 September 1944 Second British Army liberates Brussels.

4 September 1944 Second British Army liberates Antwerp.

11 September 1944 The first Allied ground forces enter Germany.

8 May 1945 V-E Day, the unconditional surrender of Germany.

8 August 1945 The Soviet Union declares war on Japan.

15 August 1945 V-J Day, the unconditional surrender of Japan.

A GUIDE TO FURTHER READING

The books and papers on the Battle of Normandy fill several rooms in libraries and archives throughout the world. But such are the controversies still surrounding the battle that there is no single, easily readable book of reasonable length that deals with the activities of all sides equally and in a straightforward and uncontroversial way. The following books give several differing viewpoints and insights into the battle. For those who wish to read further, Carlo d'Este's *Decision in Normandy* has a good bibliography.

Bellfield, E. and Essame, H. *The Battle for Normandy*, London, 1983.

Bennet, R. *Ultra in the West*, London, 1979.

d'Este, C. *Decision in Normandy*, New York and London, 1983.

Hastings, M. *Overlord – D-Day and the Battle for Normandy*, London, 1984.

Irving, D. *The War Between the Generals*, New York and London, 1981.

Keegan, J. *Six Armies in Normandy*, New York and London, 1982.

Lucas, J. and Barker, J. *The Killing Ground – the Battle of the Falaise Pocket*, London, 1978.

McKee, A. *Caen – Anvil of Victory*, London, 1984.

Ryan, C. *The Longest Day – the D-Day Story*, New York and London, 1982.

THE BATTLEFIELD TODAY

Apart from the fact that new roads have replaced some of the old railways, the countryside of Normandy has changed hardly at all since the battle. It remains an attractive tourist and farming area, visited regularly by veterans of the battle and military students, either alone or in organized tours. The most normal route to take from Britain is by ferry to Cherbourg, and a car is virtually essential for touring the battlefield.

The city of Caen has been extensively rebuilt following the Allied bombing and the destruction of the battle. In the city center is the Musée Mémorial de la Bataille de Normandie, which forms a starting place for an exploration of the battlefield. Northeast of Caen, Pegasus Bridge is still standing and clearly marked. The remains of the Mulberry harbor, unofficially named Port Winston, are still at Arromanches. Those who have lost relatives in the battle may wish to visit the British cemetery at Bayeux or the American cemetery beside "Omaha" Beach. The view from the Pointe de Hoc, which was climbed by the American Rangers, is very impressive.

Those seeking information on the battle or the battlefield in Britain may wish to contact either the Imperial War Museum, Lambeth Road, London SE1 6HZ (01-735-8922), or the D-Day Museum, Clarence Esplanade, Southsea, Portsmouth PO5 3NT (01705-827261), which also displays the famous "Overlord" Embroidery.

WARGAMING NORMANDY

The first obstacle to recreating any twentieth century battle as a wargame is the sheer scale of the exercise. The numbers of troops involved, the geographical extent of the battlefields and the logistical complications multiply rapidly the further one delves into the age of mass production and mechanization. The sprawling fluidity of modern warfare also tends to blur the line between battle and campaign, making the isolation of "manageable" conflicts more difficult, while air power adds the speed and long-range hitting power of warfare in another dimension. As a result, the following suggestions for wargaming D-Day and its immediate aftermath are best divided into two broad categories: first, the fighting of army, corps and divisional actions; and second, gaming key aspects of the battle in detail – the small-scale tactical approach.

High Command

Assuming the role of Rommel or Montgomery is a fairly daunting prospect for even the most confident of megolamaniacs, yet this level of command must be replicated if the wargamer is to fight the Normandy battles in their entirety. For warfare on this scale – assuming the lack of a convenient aircraft hangar and funds rivaling the national defense budget – miniatures are out, and maps, counters and rules that reflect high-level decision-making are in.

Fortunately, help is at hand in the form of several easily available board games, which (at a price) give the would-be gamer a ready-to-use package. The giant (in every respect) among the currently available D-Day games is *The Longest Day*, a monster of a game, whose comprehensive coverage of the events portrayed in this book is reflected in its hefty price, but whose popularity promises a satisfying and historically sound refight for those with some experience of board game rules and plenty of time. The detail in which *The Longest Day* covers D-Day is indicated by its classification as a campaign/battle game, combining the sweep of army and corps maneuvers with the actions of smaller units.

Also available is *D-Day*, a much simpler (and much cheaper) campaign-style game, and *Fortress Europa, France 1944* and *Normandy Campaign* – all, in part, dealing with post D-Day events at campaign level, the latter with the additional feature of secret map moves, which entails the need for a third party as umpire.

Four games that deal with specific battles are available. These are, in chronological order: *Omaha Beach*, the first ten days of the American V Corps's struggle to consolidate its hold on the most fiercely contested beach; *St. Lô*, the capture of the key town south of the bridgehead by American forces; *Cobra*, the American VII Corps's crucial breakout from the beachhead; and *Hitler's Counterstroke*, the Mortain counterattack that led to the annihilation of ten German divisions in the Falaise Pocket.

Valuable though the coverage of these games is, they tend to concentrate on American feats of arms and, of course, leave many other crucial actions – such as the flanking parachute drops and Operations "Epsom" and "Goodwood" – in the cold. Enterprising wargamers will see the potential here for devising their own map games, perhaps modeling them on those available commercially, but eschewing the "cheat-proof" prose of the commercial rule book for a more concise and flexible approach. This book provides the starting point for the research necessary to formulate such a game and, as those who have trodden this path will know, it is an absorbing way to learn more about the men and minutiae behind the seemingly bland "headlines" of military history.

Perhaps inspired by this research, the wargamer may then like to add another dimension to his reenactment of the Normandy battles and step rather more directly into the shoes of the senior commanders. This may be achieved by playing a game – such as *The Longest Day* – with several players on each side, forming a proper chain of command and isolating the high commands and their staffs from the all-revealing map board. This approach can range from simply placing the senior commanders in separate rooms, communicating orders and receiving information via slips of paper, to elaborate arrangements necessitating the occupation of a school or similarly large building. With careful planning and sufficient players this allows many levels of command to be simulated, with separate army, corps and divisional commanders, not to mention their airforce and naval counterparts, a small staff working under each one, and liaison officers attempting to provide the personal touch that telephoned orders and brief dispatches so often lack.

In such a game several umpires are required, not only to move the counters on the map board and resolve combats but also to regulate the flow of information to the two military hierarchies and introduce problematic "wrenches" into the works. In this manner the initial confusion of the German command can be reflected, as can the disruptive effects of multiple parachutist sightings, communication delays and the interventions of a paranoically skeptical Hitler.

A further step is to remove the map game entirely and seat the players together in what Wargames Development (the organization which also developed the "Mega Game" approach outlined above) term a Committee Game. More in line with the role-play techniques common in many science fiction and fantasy games, this is an exercise in debate and persuasion, each player being given specific goals to achieve. Properly researched, this could be an ideal way to explore the initial planning for Operation "Overlord": the selection of landing zones, the size of the assault force, the availability of landing craft and so on. Similarly, the dispositions of the defending divisions and the key question of where best to deploy the panzer forces could provide an interesting insight into the negotiations between Rommel and von Rundstedt.

Having discounted the use of miniatures (that is, model soldiers, vehicles, ships and aircraft) at high command level, one should point out that when the map movements in commercial and "homemade" games result in a clash of arms, the combat table can be replaced by a tabletop set up of terrain and models – the fighting taking place in three dimensions and being governed by an appropriate set of miniatures rules. However, the problem here again is one of scale. Even using 6mm scale armor (or the latest: 2mm!) the sheer numbers involved in the major clashes, such as the 78 88mm guns holding the line against Operation "Goodwood," are prohibitive. The answer is, of course, to scale down the forces, the normal procedure when wargaming other historical periods but strangely out of vogue in recent years where the Second World War is concerned.

A step "back" to this approach has been made by the American "Command Decision" rules and scenario system. These also favor the larger 20mm scale models (recently undergoing a renaissance, but always my firm favorites) and utilize the simple expedient of scaling down the forces involved until they become manageable. As a result, a German infantry company is represented by six model figures mounted on three "stands"; a tank company by three tanks. The rules reflect the swing away from section and squad actions to the command decisions influencing platoons, companies and above.

Tactical Games

The recent trend in Second World War tactical combat has been to represent troops and vehicles on a one-to-one basis, with 6mm (1/300th) scale miniatures proving the most popular medium. Rules such as the best-selling *Firefly* set will give an accurate and detailed game up to battalion level and, with a little care in its preparation, a tabletop representation of the notorious Normandy bocage will deliver a sobering lesson in the difficulty of piercing a dense defensive line in close country. Here again, board games provide a ready packaged alternative – especially in respect of squad- and platoon-level combat. The appropriately named *Squad Leader* and *Advanced Squad Leader* series of games are particularly popular and offer such clearly D-Day orientated scenarios as *Paratrooper* and *Hedgerow Hell*. These games, however, offer only "typical" scenarios, and the wargamer wishing to refight the numerous small actions of D-Day and its aftermath will have to suffer the satisfaction of doing his own research.

Two of the best documented small-unit "battles" are found in the activities of 6 (British) Airborne Division on the western flank of the invasion beaches. Major John Howard's gliderborne *coup-de-main* at the Orne bridges and the assault by a much reduced 9 Para (150 men) on the Merville Battery are recounted in great detail in a number of publications – often complete with maps and aerial photographs. The secret of successfully recreating these actions is to read and absorb the firsthand accounts of combat. The common combination of horror and dry wit also serves to remind the wargamer exactly whose war he is turning into *recreation*, and what those involved had to endure.

Deeper delving will provide a host of scenarios for both American and British parachutist skirmishes and "penny packet" armor support of their (and other infantry units') assaults on fortified villages and small defensive positions. The close country of the bocage and the street fighting encountered in towns such as St. Lô and Caen also lends itself to the "skirmish" approach, where one 20mm or 54mm scale soldier represents an identified personality and sections of men stalk each other in bounds or moves of just a few seconds. Detail here – if this style of game is to the taste of the wargamer – includes different severities of wound and varying skill values. Once more, real scenarios can be unearthed, such as the bizarre dash in a jeep and trailer laden with explosives by eight parachutists of 6 Parachute Division's 3rd Engineer Squadron, hell-bent on destroying a vital bridge, despite heavy German opposition.

A similar form of game can be constructed around a troop or platoon of tanks – either fighting forward through the hedgerow "maze" in support of infantry, or in the case of 79th Armored Division's "Funnies" (the specialized support tanks in the vanguard of the British and Canadian assaults) tackling the beach obstacles they were designed to neutralize, such as mines, sea walls and enemy pillboxes. A board game – *Patton's Best* – gives a flavor of D-Day armored warfare by placing a solitary player in command of a single tank and fighting it through a number of typical Western Front scenarios. In three dimensions, a large-scale tank model may fit the bill.

Often neglected when considering Normandy as a wargame subject is the business of landing (and attempting to repel) the assault troops at the water's edge. An interesting game could revolve around a company of American infantry landing from LCVPs (available in cast resin in 20mm scale) and attempting to leave the beach under heavy fire. In this "Omaha"-like situation, rules for leadership and "inspiration" would be vital. From the German point of view, a player (or players) could experience the problems of the Atlantic Wall gunners. An inverted periscope placed on the table could be used to provide a periodic view of the approaching assault vessels. By using models of different scales the bunker commander could be presented with "closing" targets – having to select which to fire at and at what ranges. The obscuring effect of Allied bombs and naval shells could be simulated, as could the players' intermittent communications with superiors and other positions.

In Conclusion

Two final points may help capture some of the flavor of D-Day on map or tabletop.

First, the nature of airpower during the period of the invasion and breakout. This was possibly the Allies' strongest card, and command of the skies meant that German movement in daylight was both slow and expensive in men and machines. In tactical games, however, it must be remembered that effective control of aircraft can only be achieved by "Tentacle" air controllers with the forward troops, and that aerial differentiation between friend and foe is notoriously difficult – especially if they are locked in combat.

Second, it should be remembered that armor was a vital, but not omnipotent, factor in the Normandy fighting. "Swimming" tanks floundered *en masse* off "Omaha" beach; Operation "Goodwood" saw 500 tanks lost to German guns sited in depth in a narrow corridor; the bocage made armor horribly vulnerable to short-range fire, and rocket-armed Typhoons terrorized (more than they destroyed) Germany's heaviest tanks. The Normandy battles were essentially decided by infantry, effectively supported by armor, artillery, aircraft and (while in range) naval gunnery.

In sum, the wargamer is well served with both information and materials for the D-Day period. Wargames figures, vehicles, aircraft and naval craft are now available in a host of scales and materials, and these are regularly advertised – along with terrain, rules and the board games mentioned in this section – in magazines such as *Wargames Illustrated*.

Prints credited to the Imperial War Museum are available on application to the Department of Photographs, Imperial War Museum, Lambeth Road, London SE1. The Visitors' Room is open to the public by appointment.